KU-527-142

TEACHERS' CENTRES

NEWMAN COLLEGE
BARTLEY GREEN
BIRMINGHAM, 32.
CLASS 370.72
ACCESSION 41989
AUTHOR THO

WITHDRAWN

TEACHERS' CENTRES

Edited by
Robert Thornbury

Darton, Longman & Todd
London

First published in Great Britain in 1973 by
Darton, Longman & Todd Limited
85 Gloucester Road, London SW7 4SU
© 1973 by Robert Thornbury, Geoffrey Matthews,
Harry Kahn, Bill Greenwood, R. G. Gough,
Janet Roseveare
Printed in Great Britain by
The Anchor Press Ltd., and bound by
Wm. Brendon, both of Tiptree, Essex
ISBN 0 232 51211 6

Contents

Acknowledgements

I would like first of all to acknowledge the permission of the Editor of *Education in Cheshire* to reproduce the illustration in Chapter 2 of the floor plan of Tarporley Teachers' Centre.

I should like to thank D. J. Johnston, of the University of London, Gordon Hamflett of the DES and Dr G. J. Copley of ILEA for giving me advice and observations. The librarians of the ILEA Education Library and Mrs O. Stokes, of the London Institute of Education Library, provided invaluable help in researching for sources and the bibliography. Mrs Clare Cheasty, my secretary, has spent many hours typing the manuscript; Mrs Lorraine Bell, my deputy, has been a great source of help; and I am grateful to Mr Brian Bowell, of Sherbrooke Centre, for his assistance with the photographs. I have appreciated the continuing support of Mr Alan Radford and Mr Howell Davies, ILEA District Inspectors, and Mr Denzil Hackford, formerly headmaster of Sherbrooke Primary School. Above all, I should like to acknowledge the dedicated professionalism of my friends and colleagues in the West London schools, especially Mr R. Kay and the staff of Sherbrooke School.

Finally, on a more personal note I want to thank my wife Mary Lou for her constant encouragement and ideas and to apologise to Clare, Jane and Paul for any play we may have missed.

Robert Thornbury

March 1973

1 *Introduction: A Tumult of Centres*

ROBERT THORNBURY

A NEW ZEALAND TEACHERS' UNION OFFICIAL, A NEW YORK elementary school principal, a sari'd administrator from Delhi, 20 Brazilian class teachers, a West German director of education, a lecturer planning the raising of the Hong Kong school-leaving age, a teaching sister from Connemara, and the education minister for a Middle East oil sheikdom – this mixed group of educationalists – visiting London in summer 1972 all made the same request. They all asked to see a teachers' centre. In fact, they all visited Sherbrooke Teachers' Centre, three converted classrooms in a Hammersmith primary school. Other teachers' centres all over the country were at the same time welcoming a similar flow of visitors.

The international interest in teachers' centres and their stunning proliferation has arisen because they are a 'British first', an idea so psychologically sound that it is a puzzle to know why they have not dotted the educational landscape for decades. They 'put the monkey of educational reform on the teachers' back'[1] as an American writer has expressed it, they meet the felt needs of teachers and show the futility of attempting educational reform without teachers being directly and importantly involved. Their rise has been phenomenal. They have irradiated so fast that even the average teacher is not fully aware of the silent educational revolution that teachers' centres have achieved.

Diagram I

Distribution of Courses for Teachers in 1966–1967, showing the Initiating Role of Local Education Authorities.

Initiating Course	% of Courses
Local Education Authorities	69·2
Universities and Institutes of Education	16·4
Colleges of Education	4·6
Department of Education and Science	1·5
Various Others	8·1

Diagram II

Location of In-Service Courses in 1966–7

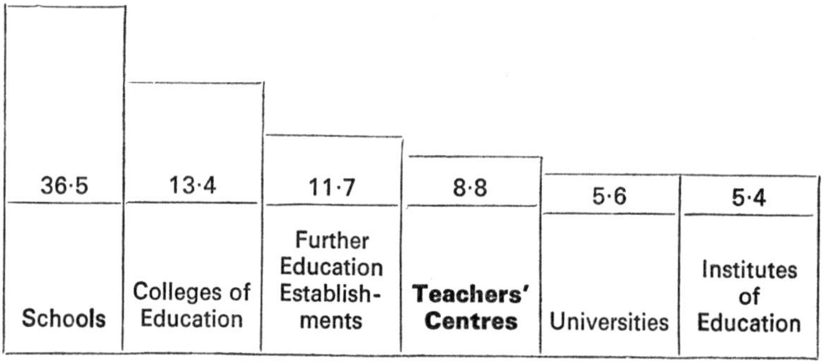

36·5	13·4	11·7	8·8	5·6	5·4
Schools	Colleges of Education	Further Education Establish-ments	**Teachers' Centres**	Universities	Institutes of Education

For teachers' centres have grown, from a mere handful in 1960, to 270 in 1967 and 450 centres in 1970. By 1972, a tumult of 617 centres could be observed in action. The post of warden had even won that golden accolade, a separate section in the job columns of the world's most widely read educational weekly *The Times Educational Supplement*. The build-up of staffing and resources which has gone on in the urban teachers' centres has made them in recent years the fastest-growing establishments in English education – at least in percentage terms. Upon my appointment in early 1969, for instance, I was a half-time warden, with no staff. By the beginning of 1973, the centre staff, including part-timers, consisted of the warden, deputy warden, two secretaries, a media resources officer, an audio-visual aids trainee and a caterer; together with a panel of more than 50 lecturers contributing on a regular basis to day and evening courses.

Contemporary origins

Teachers' centres spring from complex but identifiable origins in the British educational scene of the 1960's. 1) By the middle of that decade, the successful experience of secondary schools in developing teacher-controlled local examinations, and of primary teachers in developing in local groups the Nuffield mathematics project materials, had sparked off a mood of confident professionalism. 2) Simultaneously, there emerged across the country hundreds of new, large, comprehensive schools. These leviathans had subject departments large enough to train young staff and sufficient resources to carry on school-based curriculum development. They were their own teachers' centres. Government policy, later modified, required education authorities in the late 1960's to submit a comprehensive schools reorganisation plan. It was a novel situation, requiring endless consultation with the teachers who would work the new system. Teachers' centres were therefore provided as neutral settings where discussion could go on away from the administrative atmosphere of the education office or the charged emotional climate of a threatened school. 3) At the same time, scores of new education authorities had been created at the stroke of a pen following the reorganisation of local government itself. In this connection too, teachers' centres were deliberately set up as neutral ground where all the administrators and teachers of a locality could meet together. 4) In some decaying urban areas, a further motive in the creation of centres was the need to attract teachers to staff the schools at all. Certainly, this was the case in Birmingham, a city unable to pay a cost of living allowance to its teachers, where a large social and recreational centre giving 'fringe benefits' was established as early as 1952. 5) Exceptionally high staff turnover in the run-down urban areas also required an ongoing programme for supporting professionally the waves of young teachers who arrived each year in the schools. 6) Successive surveys had shown that the colleges of education were failing to prepare students adequately for the classroom. Many young teachers needed immediate crash courses, especially in the teaching of reading. Serving teachers were also dissatisfied with the existing provision of in-service education. Teachers' centres by putting on courses which met real needs were greeted warmly by teachers and administrators. The initiative in curriculum innovation had passed from the colleges in the post-war period to the classroom floor. The other traditional providers of in-service education, the university departments, had been too pre-occupied since 1948 with making education a respectable academic subject, thereby failing to cater for the real needs of teachers. Nor had the professional associations, sadly, shown much vigour. A few energetic local associations, such as the Monmouthshire branch of the National Union of Teachers, had a strong tradition of promoting in-service courses. But most professional associations and their members were concerned only with salary and conditions. During the 1960's matters were not helped either by the departure of those teachers most talented at curriculum development or in needing courses for posts in the expanding colleges of education and advisory staffs of LEA's. The amusing story related by Pollard is probably typical:

'Five years ago, I taught for a mercifully brief spell in an area whose local education authority stipulated that unless enough teachers signed up for the annual refresher course – held by some demonic piece of planning at the spring half-term – the half-term break (already reduced to one day for those who were refresher bound) would be cancelled. The result of this anti-professional arrangement – which was cheerfully supported by the County N.U.T. association and organisers of the course – was that most wily teachers paid their ten shillings to sign up and mysteriously failed to appear at their lectures. This story explains partly why, in writing about in-service training, I shall not be paying tribute to the role of the teachers' organisations.'[2]

7) During these years, as the educational sociologist Bryan Wilson explained in a key article,[3] British teachers were worried by an increasing sense of 'diffuseness' in their role. Many sought to compensate for this lack of clear professional identity by acquiring 'hard' teaching skills at the teachers' centres. They became experts with overhead projectors, the phonics approach to reading, or the new mathematics. 8) There was widespread public anxiety in these years about deteriorating national attainment particularly in reading, writing and spelling. Parents and teachers felt obscurely that a revival of some traditional skills and discipline was desirable. 9) Yet at the same time there was national awareness of the need to modernise the curriculum particularly in mathematics and science teaching. We had learned a lesson from the Americans who, having been shatteringly overtaken by Russian space technology, had made an agonised re-appraisal of their whole educational system. Anyway, wouldn't these new comprehensive schools need an equally new curriculum? 10) Certain political and educational decisions had been made at the national level – to raise the school leaving age, and to introduce metrication prior to joining the European Common Market – which made curriculum reform essential. 11) Teachers were in need of in-service support dealing with an incredible flood of project reports, audio-visual aids

machinery, and huge quantities of reading schemes and other books that were pouring into the schools – if these were not to lie dusty and abandoned in schoolroom cupboards. 12) At last teacher supply was improving and to some it looked as though there might be in the near future an embarrassing surplus of teachers. Was this not the time to plan schemes which would use these spare teachers to cover release for in-service education? 13) Finally, successive educational reports had urged an expansion of in-service training. The influential Plowden Committee had in particular praised highly the idea of local teachers' centres.

> 'Local centres are also invaluable in supporting the innovations introduced by individual teachers, the source of most educational progress. They ought to start from a knowledge of what local teachers are doing. They can provide opportunities for teachers to meet others who are a little ahead of themselves but whose practice is within their reach.'[4]

In-service history

Teachers have of course traditionally been concerned with their own curriculum development and in-service education. This is a point often overlooked by those critical of their five-day week and long holidays. By the early eighteenth century, as part of this long historical tradition, outstanding charity schoolmasters were already arranging courses to raise professional standards. The parent voluntary societies organised courses for serving teachers. Later, when compulsory state schooling was introduced in late Victorian England, a strong connection developed under the Revised Code between payment and results. Many school boards actually ran courses in the subjects which earned grant rewards. Consequently a cash relationship between employers and teachers was over-emphasised. This straitjacket was not effectively removed until the twentieth century, as late as 1925, when the mandatory Burnham salary structure was introduced. Another organisation active in the nineteenth century and at the present time still, the College of Preceptors, was awarded a royal charter in 1848 for the purpose of in-service training. Forty years later such interest was being shown in teaching experiments that the Educational Development Association was founded. The Monmouthshire branch of the National Union of Teachers, already mentioned, began running an annual in-service school for teachers in the early 1900's. But, as I have suggested, the professional associations did not display a good record generally.

A major embryonic step in developing the teachers' centre idea and one which seems to have escaped present-day notice was the publication of the McNair Report by the Board of Education in 1944.[5] Resulting from its recommendations, the Institute of Education and the Area Training Organisations were set up in 1948. McNair also urged the setting up of a building which could become the educational centre of an area. The Education Centre it envisaged could be used by staffs of the university, training colleges, technical colleges, colleges of art, drama and physical training – and by teachers from schools of all kinds. Striking a curiously modern note, the McNair Committee saw the education centre being used for the purpose of informal contact and formal meetings of any kind for those who mixed together there as members of the teaching profession. The centre would offer the amenities of a club and it would experiment in the development of public opinion on local educational problems. In fact only in a few places such as the London Institute of Education was even limited provision made for an education centre. As Ethel Thompson has shown in a recent, perceptive research note,[6] the education centres pictured by McNair never really got off the ground. Instead the new Area Training Organisations and Institutes became preoccupied with the raising of the status of education as a subject. 'Over emphasis on the elevation of education as an academic study and insufficient concern about practical teaching led to the neglect of suggestions made about teachers' centres in 1944.' Nor did things improve. By the 1960's the same institutions were concentrating on the vast expansion of initial training, the innovation of three-year certificate courses, B.Ed. degree courses and advanced and higher degree courses for experienced teachers – and still not on the establishment of professional centres for teachers. Even then their in-service provision was most unsatisfactory, as educational research was to show. The teachers' centres idea, as recommended by the McNair Report, remained unfulfilled, the fourth and last of its original aims. In 1968, it is true, a modified programme of more realistic DES/ATO courses for teachers was introduced. But local education authorities had gone ahead several years earlier with establishing several hundred teachers' centres of their own. The educational academics had been over-idealistic and proved too slow to deal with the immediacy of rapid educational change.

The educational research evidence for teachers' centres

In 1967 two surveys were undertaken which sharply illuminated shortcomings in the existing in-service education for teachers. A government statistical report, not finally published until 1970, presented an intriguing picture.[7] Looking at their distribution, it revealed that local education authorities initiated 70% of all courses for teachers (see diagram 1). Most courses were held in schools, further education establishments, colleges of education, or universities and their institutes – but even at that early date 8·8% of all courses were being locally sited in teachers' centres (see diagram 2). The government survey drew attention to 'the important part played even in 1966/67 by teachers' centres, where nearly 10% of all courses were held'.

Attendance at teachers' centres had occupied more than one in six teachers in the latter half of 1967. They went along to practise or discuss new materials and techniques with their colleagues. Since these figures suggested the rise of teachers' centres was a major growth point, a DES research made a special analysis of the 1, 241 teachers who attended courses at centres. They found that teachers warmly greeted the idea of a centre within easy reach of their school. Most teachers wanted to use centres either in school hours or immediately after school, but a few would even use centres at the weekends or during the school holidays. Enthusiasm for teachers' centres was equally divided between men and women, irrespective of the type of school or whether they were married or promoted. A significant minority of teachers at that time wanted the centres to provide courses leading to specific qualifications. Very few liked the idea of using centres for social contact with colleagues.

The report announced a revealing discovery:

> 'in spite of the emphasis placed by teachers learning from one another by visits, displays of work and discussion, only 4% of all teachers had taken part on the staff of in-service training courses in the previous three years.'

The same survey asked college of education lecturers what they thought about teachers' centres. College staff were strongly in favour of having a teachers' centre situated on their premises. They saw themselves using the centre for the exchange of experience and ideas with working teachers. Teachers could be involved in the planning and supervision of school practice through a college-based teachers' centre and the college would be able to maintain teacher contact with young teachers in their first year.

A second important survey in 1967, undertaken by Brian Cane for the National Foundation of Educational Research, looked at the in-service training, views and preferences, of 2,601 Durham, Norfolk and Glamorganshire teachers.[8] This survey was sponsored because of a lack of research evidence about in-service training and because some new trends had been observed. In particular, while the county residential centres, a familiar feature of British in-service training, had continued to flourish – a trend towards shorter day courses and local curriculum groups had been noticed in recent years. For the purposes of his survey Cane defined in-service training as 'all those courses and activities in which a teacher might participate in order to extend his professional knowledge, interest or skill, including preparation for further qualifications.'

The survey discovered that up to a quarter of experienced teachers had never undertaken in-service training. There was a widespread belief that in-service training was professionally desirable, few being antagonistic, but most teachers believed existing courses were not relevant to the harsh reality of classroom life. Giving their reason for not attending courses, teachers said they resented interruption in the continuity of their work with the school and children. It was difficult for suitable replacements to be found for courses during school hours and they disliked giving their colleagues extra work. How then could secondment or release be arranged for teachers, while safeguarding the interests of the school and children? Cane found that head teachers favoured short secondments of two to three weeks. Most heads were prepared to employ a supply or floating teacher for that short time, who could be attached to a small group of neighbouring schools. There was clearly scope for an expansion of the release and secondment of teachers. The problem of replacement could be solved. Further, if participation in courses was linked more with promotion half of the teachers interviewed said that they would be willing to attend. Many young, non-graduate teachers showed enthusiasm for courses leading to a B.Ed. degree.

What topics should in-service courses cover? Teachers at that time put forward nine priority areas:

1) learning difficulties
2) new methods of school and class organisation
3) new apparatus
4) planning and developing syllabuses
5) courses on recent educational research relevant to their work
6) the teaching of academic subjects to non-academic children
7) teaching large mixed-ability classes with little equipment or space

8) demonstration of new schemes of work and discussion of their results
9) instruction, marking and interpretation of exams and assessment tests

Disturbingly, an analysis of the courses actually provided by two of the three education authorities in the survey, showed virtually no attention was being given to half of these topics most in demand.

What teaching method appealed most to teachers? They favoured participation in working parties and discussion groups, observing other teachers' lessons and activities, and radio and television in-service programmes for teachers. The traditional lecture and discussion approach was roundly condemned.

How could in-service training courses be followed through by teachers in their schools? More primary teachers than secondary teachers reported that they were able to put into practice their experience from in-service courses. In-service training appeared to have had considerable impact in junior and infant schools and involvement of teachers in the Nuffield mathematics project was particularly evident (*see Chapter 4*).

A common grumble from teachers was that they were often out of pocket as the result of going to courses. They had definite preferences. They wanted in-service training close to their own home or school, ideally during school hours; otherwise at a convenient time after school, for half or a full day or at weekends or for up to one week at a time during vacations. The NFER report deduced therefore that the provision of local rather than national or regional in-service education was urgently needed. Emphasis on local courses would remove the need for residence and meet the complaints of teachers about the cost of travel and that they were too tired to travel far after a day's work.

Looking at the in-service education actually being provided in 1966/67, Brian Cane gloomily concluded that the overall picture was one of 'general poverty of provision', despite some praiseworthy efforts. The educational research evidence in both reports had pointed indisputably, however, to the need for teachers' centres.

The Schools Council monolith

If conditions were ripe by the 1960's for a major initiative, the move that triggered off events, culminating in the creation of the Schools Council, occurred in 1962. An innocent-sounding curriculum study group was set up by Sir David Eccles in his Ministry of Education. But immediately this precedent aroused widespread suspicion and hostility among teachers and local education administrators. They suspected an innovation which might quickly lead to centralised direction of the curriculum. Some feared that a continental system, derived from the Napoleonic Code, was just round the corner – soon all children of nine years old would be busy conjugating a particular verb at a given time in the morning on a given day of the year. As the result of vociferous protest, a committee under Sir John Lockwood was set up instead to review matters. The curriculum study group proved to have had a short life.

In its place was proposed the Schools Council, a new and independent organisation in which the Secretary of State for Education, local education authorities and teachers would act as partners, but with a majority of teachers serving on its main committees. This turn of events meant that from 1964 onwards the teachers' professional associations were to dominate national curriculum policies, at the Schools Council – the national teachers' centre – a fact not generally appreciated. At local level, on the other hand, as I have indicated, professional association interest was to run at a low ebb for the first decade.

The report of the Lockwood Committee in concerning itself with the aims and constitution of the Schools Council was emphatically clear. Teachers should be completely free to choose for themselves in curriculum matters. Publications of the Schools Council, for instance, would carry no authority whatever apart from their own intrinsic merit.

The educational monolith which had suddenly emerged rapidly captivated the imagination of major public figures of the day. Its first chairman was Sir John Maud, an eminent civil servant known to millions through his television appearances. In 1966, however, Maud was called to chair a royal commission on local government. Alan Bullock, another television don, at that time author of a widely read book on Hitler, was asked to take over. Readers opening the first issue of *Dialogue*, house journal of the Schools Council, were told of Bullock's excitement at being asked to take on the job.

> 'It was an impulsive decision, I remember standing in an unlighted village call box on a wet night (the conference was meeting in a Hertfordshire country house) ringing up my wife to tell her what I proposed to do. Her first question was one that was to become all too familiar in the next two years: "but what is the Schools Council?" Her comment when I told her put my own feelings in a single sentence: "it's not what it is, it's what it might become".'[9]

Despite demurrals, those addicted to the conspiracy theory of history might be forgiven for wondering whether a full-scale state coup d'état of curriculum was not part of the original design.

For a time the government maintained the Schools Council, providing staff, administration and running costs together with some funds for projects. But as soon as government accountants could devise a mechanism for them to deduct a relevant sum from the rate support grant, the local authorities began to make their contribution. This took several years to arrange. During that time the Nuffield Foundation held out in the way described by Geoffrey Matthews in Chapter 4. By 1969/70, setting aside running costs, the DES was contributing £100,000 annually and local education authorities between them £575,000. The Gothic proliferation of Schools Council projects and activities is discussed later. It is worth noting though that by 1972 this national teachers' centre and state publishing house was handling a massive budget of £1¾m annually and supporting nearly 100 projects.

No organisation has self-respect until it is installed in its own building. After its creation in 1964 the Schools Council became bureaucratically well established in London in Great Portland Street, conveniently near the BBC, the University of London and, of course Whitehall. The monolith was ready to lurch into print.

The scene was set for an educational explosion. This is just what took place, as within eight years more than 600 teachers' centres invaded the English educational map. So much was to happen, so quickly, that there were complaints that, far from a general 'poverty of provision', in-service education had arrived over-abundantly. 'Course notices pour into schools like travel brochures into the homes of would-be holiday makers',[10] a writer was to announce in the Lent 1972 issue of the *Cambridge Journal of Education.*

1. Bailey, Stephen K., *Teachers' Centres: A British First*, Phi Delta Kappan, Vol. 53, No. 3, November 1971, pp. 146–9.
2. Pollard, Michael, *Soft Centres*, In-service Training, Education and Training, Vol. 12, October 1970, pp. 380–1, 386.
3. Wilson, Bryan, *The Teacher's Role – A Sociological Analysis*, British Journal of Sociology, Vol. XIII (1), 1962, pp. 15–32.
4. *Children and their Primary Schools* (Plowden Report), Vol. 1, p. 359, H.M.S.O.
5. *Teachers and Youth Leaders* (McNair Report), Board of Education, 1944, p. 59.
6. Thompson, Ethel M., *Teachers' Centres: Why they were established by Local Education Authorities instead of Institutes of Education*, Durham Research Review, Vol. 6, No. 29, Autumn 1972, p. 679.
7. Statistics of Education Special Series, No. 2, H.M.S.O. 1970, Part 1: Statistics Division of DES, Parts II & III: Townsend, H.E.R.
8. Cane, Brian, *In-service Training: A Study of Teachers' Views and Preferences*, NFER, 1969.

9. Bullock, Alan, Dialogue. Schools Council Newsletter, No. 1, September 1968, p. 3.
10. Lovegrove, W. R., *Some problems involved in in-service education*, Cambridge Journal of Education, Vol. 2, No. 1, Lent 1972, pp. 42–9.

2 *'The Fastest Vehicle in a Vacuum is a Band-Wagon . . .'*

ROBERT THORNBURY

Campaign for teachers' centres

Soon a spate of working papers and reports began to issue from Great Portland Street with a recurring propaganda theme. It was the idea of a national network of teachers' centres. Taking an ecclesiastical stance, the Schools Council claimed spiritual but not lay jurisdiction over the new centres it proposed. It did not wish to be involved in their day-to-day running, appointing staff or determining their programme. The centres would not impose a new curriculum on the schools but provide a service in response to the demands of teachers for faster progress. A small number of field officers, teachers seconded to the Schools Council, were each given a curriculum bishopric, a large area of England and Wales. The field officers were to have a special role in promoting the spread of teachers' centres. 'The teachers' centres and the Schools Council provide you with a new and exciting opportunity for your professional development', *Dialogue* informed teachers.[1]

One factor favouring the rise of centres has been mentioned as the raising of the national school-leaving age. This task, the Schools Council decided at an inaugural meeting in 1964, should be given early priority in any programme. Its second publication, therefore, immediately seized on the theme of developing teachers' centres in connection with ROSLA.[2] Local development centres should be set up, based on schools, where teachers could think through the problems of ROSLA, arriving at solutions which they could apply with real conviction.

The professional aim of these development centres would be a study by local teachers of the major areas of the curriculum, perhaps assisted by outside experts, followed by the preparation of new courses.

Teachers' centres in separate premises were not suggested at this time. Furthermore, Working Paper 2 was addressed at secondary and not the primary teachers who later proved the most enthusiastic audience. But it did spell out in detail that modest staffing and resources would be needed if time set aside for serious thinking by teachers about the curriculum was to be profitably spent. Sensitive where the LEA's, its paymasters, were concerned, the Council diplomatically preached the parable of the widow's mite.

'. . . Many authorities have provided excellent teachers' centres in existing programmes at very little cost by an imaginative use of spare accommodation in existing buildings, and even a spiritual centre operating from the leader's or secretary's own school is better than no centre at all.'

Although the council did not wish to discourage radical experiment, realistic projects and not ambitious schemes of work should be attempted.

As will become apparent later, the Schools Council was never the mouthpiece of the DES. But co-operation was evident concerning the development of teachers' centres: DES support would be given in staffing.

'The Council appreciates the difficulties at a time of teacher shortage, but education authorities might like to know that the Department of Education and Science has already agreed that one authority that is establishing a pilot scheme need not count against the quota the teachers released for this purpose.' The DES would give a similar ruling for other local authorities wishing to set up teachers' centres. The green light was flashing, a surprising concession at a time of economic squeeze. Some local authorities, concluded Working Paper No. 2, might combine in co-operative projects supported by joint resources. An account of such an experiment is given by Bill Greenwood in Chapter 6.[3]

A third Schools Council working paper, in 1965, looking at the teaching of English in relation to ROSLA, also pressed for the setting up of local development centres.[4] Although English teaching was essentially 'personal', it saw scope for co-operatively organised work. By now, some thought was being given to the primary teacher. Whatever solution was adopted, declared the working paper, individual English centres would need to bring together primary and secondary teachers as well as university staffs and advisers.

The little red pamphlet

So far the teachers' centre idea had been associated with some particular curriculum problem, such as ROSLA or the new mathematics. With the publication of Working Paper 10 in 1967, the Schools Council embarked on a campaign of exhortation.[5] Teachers' centres were intrinsically good – every authority should have one! This little red pamphlet prompted shockwaves of administrative activity and a rash of centres was soon to appear.

Working Paper No. 10 listed the facilities needed to support new work in curriculum development, but it stressed that centres could also be used for other purposes, including in-service training. Through the literature on teachers' centres runs a distinction, sometimes reflected in the noticeboards outside the actual buildings themselves, between curriculum development and in-service training. Most of the time these are phrases describing the same thing, as I shall illustrate. Part of the fascination of the warden's job is acting as a catalyst in the alchemy when courses transmute into curriculum-development and vice versa.

Working Paper No. 10, however, declared that the Schools

Council's main concern was with curriculum development in centres, new thinking by teachers themselves in reappraising their own work and that of others. Co-operative enterprise had been notably successful in the construction of CSE syllabuses and in the Nuffield Mathematics Project (described by Geoffrey Matthews in Chapter 4), when large numbers of teachers had voluntarily participated. Although CSE work had not demanded special accommodation, workshop settings had been provided in the Nuffield Project so that teachers could experiment with new materials in their own time.

The little red pamphlet asserted that effective local leadership would be essential in the network of centres it proposed. For this to happen, a steering committee reflecting local teacher opinion should be set up. How representation was to be arranged was not made entirely clear, but, said the working paper explicitly, there should be 'no hierarchy of initiative or control'. Practical questions were answered that administrators might want to ask. How many teachers should each centre serve? This would vary according to local geography, but a centre for less than 400 teachers would be uneconomic and one serving more than 800 would be overloaded. Centres should be based on an existing institution since this gave access to better facilities. Centres would be most regularly used in the evenings. One full-time leader who could be employed 'off-quota' would be needed for any centre in full operation. Part-time leaders of curriculum development groups might be appointed later.

What was the position in Wales and Scotland? In Wales, said Working Paper No. 10, different educational, cultural, economic and social factors made it advisable that local authorities, rather than proceed independently, should combine with the University of Wales. Scotland, which was outside the terms of reference of the Schools Council, presented a separate picture again. There was already a national committee of in-service education for its 3,180 schools. Curriculum development had made slow progress in Scotland because, Nisbet has suggested, the educational system was authoritarian at heart, and it was unrealistic to expect teachers to do anything other than wait for a strong lead from the centre.[6]

Make the teacher pay

The proposals for a national teachers' centre network seem like grass-roots radicalism when set against contemporary academic thinking. Higher educationists were out of touch. The most inspired scheme that could be dreamed up at the time, one which seriously suggested that teachers should pay for their own in-service education, was floated in the *British Journal of Educational Studies* for 1967.[7] Its author had observed the alarm of head teachers, where teachers' centres had been active, at what they considered to be interference in their staff training. Schools were not suitable settings in which to hold courses for teachers. Specialised accommodation, similar to the staff colleges of the armed forces, was needed. A staff college network could offer in-service education in a form appropriate to a self-governing profession and a varied programme could include courses for managers, governors, ancillary staff, social and psychological workers and even sixth formers. But who would pay? The teachers would, of course, declared Edmonds. He who called the tune must be prepared to pay the piper – it was the cost of self-government. A simple covenant deducting two guineas a year from each teacher's pay would provide the capital!

Indeed some authorities had already embarked on the staff college approach. In the progressive West Riding the tradition of residential courses stretched back to the early years of the century was consolidated in 1952 by the opening of Woolley Hall, an attractive building set aside for the purpose.[8] The Inner London Education Authority purchased a country manor house on the riverside at Stoke d'Abernon in Surrey and opened it in 1966 as a residential teachers' centre. Janet Roseveare has explained (Chapter 8) how the Cornwall Education Authority, having widely scattered schools, made the residential centre its main strategy, using hotels in different seaside towns each winter, like the roving medieval university. What Edmonds' plan failed to take account of was the demand for 'grass roots' local centres.

Inspirational centres

In 1967 the Schools Council published a summary of 40 of its reports and working papers.[9] An encouraging statistical trend was recorded. Teachers' centres were proliferating, with 137 already active and another 125 centres at the planning stage. At an international curriculum conference that year at Oxford J. G. Owen, joint secretary at the Schools Council, announced that the serving teacher had become the dominant figure in the British system for curriculum reform in innovation.[10] Conference members returned to their countries, their ears ringing with the news that 'inspirational' teachers' centres were in full flood of development in Britain.

An automatic carillon of references to teachers' centres could now be expected in any Schools Council publication. Hard on the heels of the little red pamphlet which had advocated a national network of teachers' centres, came a working paper looking at the humanities programme for ROSLA.[11] Again the formation was urged of local development groups of secondary teachers. Once more, LEA's were exhorted to provide rooms or even a complete redundant school building. The world's largest education authority, ILEA, with 20,000 teachers and 1,100 schools, forecast in 1967 developments likely to occur in London in the next few years.[12] ILEA was committed to helping teachers with buildings, apparatus and secretarial assistance in two types of centres. A network of permanent multipurpose centres, one in each of ten geographical divisions, was being provided to save teachers' travelling time in attending short courses. Simultaneously, a complex of subject centres was being located where there was interest in a particular subject or where curriculum development was to be initiated. Subject meetings were often taking place in schools and an enterprising group of English centres, based on the departments of large comprehensive schools, was established at this time.

The national picture

The enthusiastic response of teachers to the new centres, discovered by the DES and NFER surveys separately conducted in 1967, has already been mentioned. In fact there was felt to be a large enough readership emerging of teachers and others interested in curriculum development to justify launching a new publication. The first issue of the *Journal of Curriculum Studies* appeared in November 1968.

The strong impetus contributed to the origins of teachers' centres by the rapid spread of educational technology in the schools has been noted. The magazine *Visual Education* reported in 1968 on the Springbank Teachers' Centre at Leeds, where a consortium of Leeds, Wakefield and York teachers and administrators met regularly to co-ordinate in-service plans for the area.[13] A curriculum development committee at the Springbank Centre, drawing in the local Institute and colleges of education, had promoted a joint project on team teaching. A film library serving the schools in all three authorities had been organised. Similar developments were reported from Hull, where an Education Centre displayed audio-visual aids, advised would-be purchasers, provided a loan service, supported in-service courses and ran a small reprographic factory for teachers.[14]

Teachers' centre provision was under way in Wales by 1968. In nearby Shropshire, teachers had been making do with 'spiritual' centres on existing school premises but, announced the DES *Trends in Education*, the education authority was now planning proper local centres.[15]

By 1969 the explosive growth of teachers' centres was almost literally occurring. An unexploded bomb was found in the teachers' centre at Grimsby, formerly a civil defence post, just before its official opening, and the army experts had to be called in.[16] The Schools Council campaign for a national network of teachers' centres was continued unabashed. In each new issue of *Dialogue*, the Schools Council house journal, a regular column which was later dropped, 'Round and About the

Teachers' Centres', recorded the appearance of half a dozen teachers' centres. Yet another chairman of the Council, Dame Muriel Stewart, declared in its pages 'our aim must be that no teacher is without an opportunity to use a teachers' centre'.[17] A series of national conferences, sponsored by the Council, on curriculum development in teachers' centres was advertised. The Council also published in 1969 two anonymous accounts of teachers' centres.[18, 19] One of them described a centre where a teachers' development group concerned with ROSLA decided their own programme of work and even the furniture and equipment for the centre. Strangely, the click of the turnstile seemed to be the criterion by which success was measured. The chairman of one of the development groups commented proudly that he had recently visited the centre to find all the rooms fully used.

The interest of educational journalists in anything new was reflected in the coverage given by the *Teachers' World* to teachers' centres in 1969. *Teachers' World* visited and photographed a centre in North Yorkshire specialising in environmental studies.[20] It visited the Newham centre and interviewed the energetic warden, Ernest Millington.[21] He told *Teachers' World* that his job was a matter of supply and demand. The teacher only had to shout and a course was provided. Anyone seeking direction would be disappointed at Newham however, for the traditional concept of authority was being diminished in the centre.

Teachers' World was least impressed by arrangements at Epsom in Surrey, where the teachers' centre was placed in a school.[22] As in Dorset and Devon, and many other counties at that time, the Surrey centre leaders were primary heads combining two jobs usually with success but at great personal cost. In Surrey it was the practice to transfer centres to another school if the dual role proved unsatisfactory. Although the Surrey teachers were not uncritical of this arrangement, they felt there were strong compensations where a teachers' centre shared a school building. One important advantage was that children were available to co-operate with lecturers. Having personal experience of such a centre, I'm sure the Surrey teachers weren't just whistling in the dark. Any teachers' centre situated in a school, where footballs bounce against the window, where the warden turns out with children for fire drill,

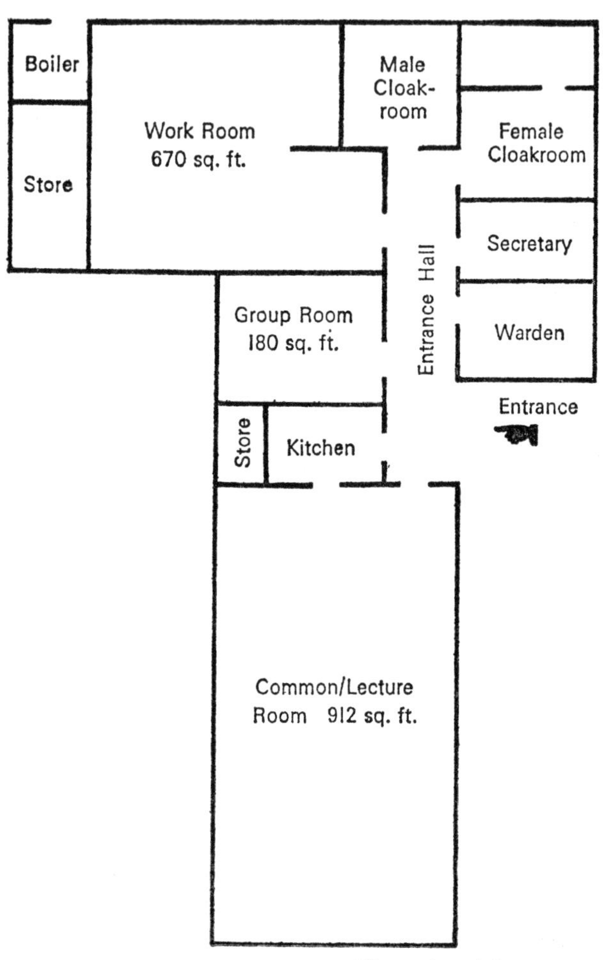

Floor plan of the centre

has lunch with them and shares a staffroom with their teachers – must be a place where realism prevails.

But wouldn't a suitable building really be necessary? In 1969 the periodical *Education in Cheshire* reported that Tarporley would be one of the few places to have a purpose-built teachers' centre (see diagram opposite).[23] Situated in the pleasing grounds of a county secondary school, the three main rooms of the Tarporley centre were to serve 1,000 teachers. As well as the usual range of teachers' centre activities, it was planned to set up a dining club where prominent educationalists would speak. There would also be a community role, for the Tarporley centre was planning exhibitions and evenings for parents. A small number of other authorities at this time developed purpose-built centres. Unfortunately, any calculations on which provision was likely to be based were soon outdated by the rate at which in-service education was expanding. No DES architect was ever able to sit down and devise cost limits or site standards for the perfect teachers' centre, circumstances changed so much. Practically any building – youth club, aerodrome, civil defence post, family house, evening institute, former sports pavilion or even an old town hall – proved suitable for teachers' centre activity. Patterns of provision varied enormously too. School reorganisation in Wigan demanded the provision of a team of advisers in a teachers' centre: while in the North-West of England a chain of curriculum development centres was set up by a consortium of LEA's to support work by teachers on the raising of the school-leaving age.

'The fastest vehicle in a vacuum is a band-wagon'

By autumn 1969 the colleges and departments of education had begun to look out of their ivory towers at the growth of teachers' centres. D. J. Johnson, the Adviser to Teachers in the Institute of Education at London, advised the colleges to set up teachers' centres of their own as had been done at the Rachel McMillan College and St John's College, York.[24] In Essex, tutor organisers had been appointed at two colleges of education, who were visiting the schools and as members of teacher committees were helping to devise the in-service programme. But most colleges remained somnambulised by their own internal rigidities and the flatulence induced by over-rapid expansion.

One of the origins of teachers' centres, it has been explained, was growing public and professional concern among parents and industrialists as well as teachers about national educational standards. The rise of the Centre for the Teaching of Reading at the University School of Education, Reading, provides a most remarkable illustration of this point. Established two years previously to help local teachers, lecturers and students, by 1970 the Reading centre had become one of the most heavily visited teachers' centres in the country, with busloads of teachers descending on it daily. Housing a permanent display of apparatus for the teaching of reading, it also offered courses, published book lists and information about reading tests and arranged exhibitions. After three years of existence it had received more than 13,000 visitors and had achieved a national status. A survey undertaken by the centre at Reading in 1970 revealed that teachers' centres all over the country were leading a new wave of professional activity designed to improve the teaching of reading.[25] Several local education authorities were planning to open their own specialist centres. As a conference wit remarked of teachers' centres, 'the fastest vehicle in a vacuum is a band-wagon'.[26]

Teachers' centres continued to have an important role in Schools Council national projects. Whenever possible, projects were constructed so that right from the start numerous groups of teachers were involved. In the Mathematics for the Majority Project, writing groups of teachers met at teachers' centres. The Middle Years of Schooling Project enlisted the help of 82 teachers' centres, whose reports provided the basis for the final publication, a working paper issued by the Schools Council.[27]

More than 440 teachers' centres were listed by the Schools Council in 1970 using information supplied by LEA's.[28] Some writers, like Pollard, were sceptical about these official statistics.

'If, however, you are honest, you would have to admit that most of these centres are, in fact, classrooms, which with no change of furniture or facilities, miraculously stopped being classrooms and start being teachers' centres on the last stroke of the four o'clock bell. You would have to add that a number of the full-time centres are housed in buildings that have been condemned as unfit for children to learn in but then given a new lease of life as places for teachers to learn in. You would also have to admit that so far from being places of the teacher's own, teachers' centres have been virtually taken over by the local education authority inspectorate without whose permission neither the warden nor the committee of teachers and stool-pigeons dares make a move.'[29]

What was the attitude towards teachers' centres of that permanent body of educational civil servants, Her Majesty's Inspectorate? Michael Birchenough, himself an HMI, wrote in the issue of *Dialogue* celebrating a centenary of state education that teachers' centres had an important part to play; in many cases HMI's had joined in the centres' teams of teachers developing new curriculum content.[30]

Report on three conferences

In 1970 was published a report of three conferences concerning teachers' centres which had just been held by the Schools Council and attended by wardens and administrators.[31] Survey material collected two years previously, and given in the conference report, showed that the time spent in centres on Schools Council projects was insignificant compared with the range of other activities being undertaken by teachers' centres. Centres had been meeting more fundamental needs. 308 authorities had set up centres by 1968. Of those 113 had been based on primary schools, but had the exclusive use of at least one room. There had been 89 centres specialising in Schools Council or Nuffield projects in mathematics, science or modern languages.

Mostly centres were controlled by the teachers, who outnumbered local education officials and politicians on management panels. But control of subject centres had been more often in the hands of LEA advisers. Although a wide range of activities was being promoted by teachers' centres, only in a minority of centres was there any systematic local curriculum development.

Local circumstances were the key factor in determining provision. Some centres served as few as 22 teachers, while others as many as 8,000. The terminology of leadership was diverse, including director, warden, teacher in charge, co-ordinator, teacher-adviser, consultant teacher, administrative officer, development assistant and secretary.

The majority of those attending the three conferences were administrators seeking a blueprint for teacher centre organisation in their own county, borough or city. They were no doubt puzzled at the conflicting range of choices opened up to them by the survey results.

An equally wide range of issues, arising from the working experience of those in existing teachers' centres, was ventilated at the three conferences.

What was the role of the warden? Often, he was a general dog's-body with duties ranging from summarising Schools Council working papers to washing up the cups and saucers. Certainly he needed many talents. He needed expertise in group discussion, behavioural psychology, curriculum planning, educational sociology, and the resources and information needed by teachers – but his real concern was as a consultant in curriculum development. Wardens were spending a good deal of their time as professional communicators, using a variety of means, including the regular newsletters, items in education bulletins, letters to individual teachers, displays at the centre and travelling exhibitions. Head teachers were a decisive group in ensuring the success of any centre and the warden's most effective method of communication was by visiting heads and teachers in their schools.

The Venus fly-trap

The conference disputed medievally the distinction between in-service training and curriculum development. Their deliberations were reminiscent of the schoolmen's quodlibet, 'How many angels can dance on the head of a pin?' Nevertheless it was an important issue. Curriculum development was, in jargon, 'defining the aims and objectives of teaching, constructing appropriate methods and materials, assessing their effectiveness, and feeding back results of their use to provide a starting point for a further cycle'. In-service training, on the other hand, was the retail side of the business, concerned with selling the successful result to the consumer through courses. The higher good was always curriculum development, and always the aim should be to convert any course into a curriculum development group. Teachers' centres were therefore a Venus fly-trap where the colour and scent of courses lured teachers on to the sticky surface of curriculum development.

Conference members held divided views over the future of teachers' centres. Some 'grass roots' theorists wanted the control of local development to remain entirely in the hands of teachers. Others thought this was naive – the stimulus of national projects in established courses of training would be essential. Bureaucrats were preoccupied with the minutiae of teachers' centre provision, asking again and again for minor facilities. Evangelists, eschewing worldly goods such as electric tea-urns and typewriters, stressed the 'inspirational' nature of teachers' centre activity. It was the congregation and not the building which made up the church.

How could secondary teachers be attracted to the centres? The secondary head teacher was a managerial figure and the heads of department were the key figures in large schools with whom centres should make contact. Interest was stirring by 1970 in the idea of teachers' centres as resource collections. One or two conference speakers wanted production facilities as well as audio-visual aids and print library services provided by the centres. The conference brought out clearly the paradox that local centres were not proving local at all. Difficulties in travel were being experienced, both in rural areas where long journeys had to be made on minor roads, and in the cities where traffic congestion meant a teacher might waste an hour travelling just a few miles.

The chief difficulty obstructing the further development of teachers' centres was declared on all sides, however, to be the release of teachers. Suggestions were made for solving the problem in three ways: by timetabling arrangements, by the use of replacement staff, or contractually. Some thought that team-teaching and scientific timetabling would make easier the release of teachers. Perhaps a pool of replacement staff, peripatetic supply teachers or students, could be used. Or teachers could be redeployed on a three-session day in secondary schools, involving the youth service and further education staff. The teacher's contract might also be altered to include officially some commitment of time during the year for in-service education. Here the dichotomy between in-service training and curriculum development again reared its head. Everyone agreed that straightforward arrangements could be made to release teachers for in-service training courses. But it was essential that teachers volunteered for curriculum development. Besides, who could forecast what demands it would make on their time?

The James enquiry announced

Towards the end of 1970 circumstances changed abruptly. A new Secretary of State for Education, Mrs Margaret Thatcher, announced her immediate intention of setting up a small, high-powered investigation into all teacher training. A committee of seven people led by Lord James of Rusholme was instructed to report within a year. Two other enquiries into teacher education, proceeding at a leisurely pace at that time, were pushed aside. The Minister wanted speed and decisiveness. The James committee was given a broad remit. They were asked to say whether intending teachers should be educated with other students, and to define the future role of the colleges of education, polytechnics and other educational establishments including the universities themselves.

1. Rogers, G. A., *The Teacher and the Council.* Dialogue. Schools Council Newsletter, No. 1, September 1968, p. 4.
2. *Raising the School Leaving Age,* Schools Council Working Paper, No. 2, H.M.S.O., 1965, see pages 32 and 24.
3. Rudd, W. G. A., *The North West Curriculum Development Project,* Forum, Spring 1968, Vol. 10, No. 2.
4. *English: A Programme for Research and Development in English Teaching.* Schools Council Working Paper, No. 3, H.M.S.O., 1965.
5. *Curriculum Development: Teachers' Groups and Centres,* Schools Council Working Paper, No. 10, see p. 8.
6. Nisbet, J., *Curriculum Development in Scotland,* Journal of Curriculum Studies, Vol. 2, No. 1, May 1970, pp. 5–10.
7. Edmonds, E. L., *Education for Responsibility, Fifty Teacher Staff Colleges,* British Journal of Educational Studies, Vol. 15, No. 3, October 1967, pp. 243–52.
8. Milne, I. R., *Woolley Hall, The West Riding Centre for In-service Training,* Froebel Journal, No. 3, October 1965, pp. 28–31.
9. *The New Curriculum* (A selection from Schools Council Publitions 1964/67), H.M.S.O., 1967.
10. Maclure, Stuart J., *Curriculum Innovation in Practice,* H.M.S.O., 1968, see p. 16.
11. *Society and the Young School Leaver: A Humanities Programme in Preparation for the Raising of the School Leaving Age,* H.M.S.O., 1967.
12. Inner London Education Authority, Education Committee Minutes, December 1967.
13. Curry, W., *The Organisation of a Teachers' Centre: Spring Bank Teachers' Centre, Leeds,* Visual Education, December 1968, pp. 10–13.
14. Mostyn, S., *Teaching Aids and the Education Centre,* Aspects of Education, No. 11, September 1970, pp. 29–31.
15. Henry, J. W., *In-service Training in Shropshire,* Trends in Education, No. 9, January 1968, p. 38.

16. Dialogue. Schools Council Newsletter, No. 3, June 1969, p. 15.
17. Stewart, Dame Muriel, *A Look ahead by the new Chairman.* Dialogue. Schools Council Newsletter, No. 4, p. 3.
18. *First Year.* An account of the Work of a Teachers' Centre, Schools Council Pamphlet, No. 1, 1969.
19. *Foundation Stones 1966–68.* An account by the Field Officers of the first two years' work of local curriculum development groups in a county authority, Schools Council, 1969.
20. Teachers' World, 24 January 1969, p. 14.
21. Teachers' World, 21 March 1969, p. 7.
22. Teachers' World, 18 July 1969, p. 20.
23. Wilson, R. C., *Tarporley Teachers' Centre,* Education in Cheshire, Spring 1969, p. 17.
24. Johnston, D. J., *In-service Evolution,* Education for Teaching, Autumn 1969, p. 6.
25. Goodacre, Elizabeth J., *Provision for Reading,* University of Reading School of Education Centre for the Teaching of Reading, 1971.
26. *Teachers' Centre Leaders in the South-West,* Themes in Education, No. 11, p. 4, Conference Report, University of Exeter Institute of Education.
27. *The Middle Years of Schooling from 8–13,* Schools Council Working Paper, No. 22, H.M.S.O., 1969.
28. *List of Teachers' Centres in England and Wales,* Schools Council, April 1970.
29. Pollard, M., *Soft Centres,* In-service Training Education, Vol. 12, October 1970, pp. 380–1, 386.
30. Birchenough, Michael, *H.M.I. and change in the Schools,* Supplement to Dialogue, Schools Council Newsletter, No. 5, February 1970, p. 15.
31. *Teachers' Centres and the Changing Curriculum: A Report on Three National Conferences,* Schools Council Pamphlet, No. 6, 1970, see p. 23.

3 *James and his White Paper*

ROBERT THORNBURY

The bandwagon gathers momentum

Some sections of the educational press awoke at last from deep slumber, following the authorising of the James Report. By mid-1971, the editorial desk at *The Teacher*, the weekly newspaper of the NUT, finally perceived the important growth of teachers' centres.[1] No doubt feeling that a proprietorial air might cover up its lack of interest in teachers' centres until that point, *The Teacher* asked what had caused the sudden rise of centres 'heralded by the National Union of Teachers as the most significant breakthrough in teacher education, but for which a decade ago there appeared to be no need'. *The Teacher* was anxious to play down any suggestion that centres might wield influence in educational politics or in awarding professional recognition for in-service work. Wardens, it declared, were opposed to courses at centres giving paper qualifications, since these might attract the wrong kind of person, the ambitious promotion-seeking teacher, rather than the average class-teacher who wanted to get on with the job. Teachers' professional associations did use centres for meetings and annual dances, but the custom was to exclude teacher-politics.

Belatedly the NUT was climbing on the bandwagon. The

journals of other professional associations were even slower off the mark – many of them still would not have carried a major article on teachers' centres by 1973.

The Times Educational Supplement had also learned by 1971, presumably from the manager of its classified columns, that teachers' centres were proliferating at a remarkable rate. How had this happened during a period of severe economic restraint, asked the TES, splashing out with a photo centre-page spread?[2] The James Committee was likely to recommend expanded use of teachers for reorganised in-service education – but what were they really like? The TES gave an encouraging picture of several teachers' centres its staff writer had visited, but pointed out that there were critics. Some saw teachers' centres as just places for a refreshing breather from school, a cup of tea, a little gentle study of the curriculum, and a shop around the latest hardware and teaching equipment, 'a sort of Lyons' Corner House'.

Ironically, the TES contrasted the York and District Curriculum Development Centre and its nearby Cinderella partner, the York Teachers' Centre. The Development Centre, supported financially by York and the three Ridings of Yorkshire as well as by a charitable grant, was a joint enterprise inspired in 1967 by the raising of the school-leaving age. It was situated in a university building by the walls of the old city and teachers were able to enjoy there some of the cloistered calm and civilised chat of academic life. The co-ordinator was specific about his aims, he was concerned only with curriculum development undertaken by working parties of teachers on day-release. There was a marked lack of glamour by contrast, reported the TES staff writer, about the York Teachers' Centre itself. 'Hidden away behind a dingy tennis court' in the grounds of the local college of education, it had no cafeteria, no common-room and no bar – although its warden, too, regarded his functions as curriculum development and in-service training.

After a slow start, *Trends in Education*, a journal issued by the Department of Education and Science, gave consistent coverage to teachers' centres. In 1971 it depicted a typical programme of activities at the Newham Centre, already mentioned, which included: working parties on children's talk, the reconstruction of an infants' classroom in the teachers' centre, and the collection by public appeal of 3,000 slides.[3] Juxtaposed in the same issue, was an account of a teachers' centre in Maryland, USA. An experimental venture in which the University, the State Education Department and the school board had co-operated, the teachers' centre there was a school or cluster of schools headed by a co-ordinator, whose salary was paid equally by the college and the schools system. There were problems similar to those emerging in Britain. Some head teachers saw centre activity as a threat to them. Some teachers did not want to be involved at all. It had not always been easy to agree on policy; and there had been problems of professional demarcation between colleges, teachers and the local community – whose voice was traditionally strong in the USA schools system.

Progress in Wales was reported, in *The Teacher in Wales*, as part of the flurry of interest in teachers' centres during the James enquiry.[4] A writer there argued against any narrow view of teachers' centres as places exclusively for curriculum development. A more general role for teachers was urged, especially in those sparsely populated areas of rural Wales remote from the university college centres. Readers were reminded that the Gittings Report, on Welsh primary education, had warned a teacher could be out of touch with educational development within five years of leaving college. At local centres, advocates of change and new ideas could be given a soap-box, and no teacher then need feel isolated from the main-stream of educational advance. While there had been sensibly no attempts to impose a pattern of identikit teachers' centres on the profession, nevertheless their spread should be encouraged.

The formation of the first regional association of teachers' centre wardens, Wardens in the South-East of England (WISE), was announced in 1971. The secretary explained in a letter published in the educational press that its aims were to exchange information and to ensure adequate expression of the views of wardens about future developments in in-service education. In conjunction with the Adviser to Teachers at the University of Education, WISE sponsored the first national conference of wardens of teachers' centres in London that summer.[5]

Mrs Thatcher's Christmas lunch

The report on Teacher Education and Training presented to the Secretary of State in time for her Christmas lunch in December 1971, was promptly christened 'the James tricycle'.[6] Teachers, declared the report, should be professionally educated in three consecutive stages: personal education, pre-service training and induction, and in-service education. Committee members placed strongest emphasis on their recommendations concerning in-service education. The James Report proposed that new regional bodies linked with a national council should administer teachers education. Serving teachers should be more directly involved in professional training. In-service training should begin in the schools.

Noting the recent expansion of in-service activity, including the growth of teachers' centres, the report prophesied heavy future demand for in-service courses leading to degrees. Arrangements should be flexible, however, formal academic courses would not always be best. For careers teachers, for instance, a spell in local industry might prove a worthwhile alternative to a conventional course. The national teacher supply had improved and high priority should now be given to providing staffing for revised schemes of in-service release. All teachers should in future be entitled to release, or secondment, on full pay for one term of in-service education, or its equivalent, in each seven years. This professional right, part of each teacher's contract, would represent the release of 5% of the teaching force at any one time.

Significantly for the teachers' centres, the James Report recommended that the entitlement should not cover evening, weekend or vacation courses or other short-term activities which might or might not involve release from school.

'Many teachers already give up their own time to attend

courses designed to improve their professional competence. There is no doubt that they would continue to do so.' Yet the development of longer, full-time courses, said the report, should not be bought at the expense of the valuable short-term activities. Indeed, it recommended that as much money as was currently spent on the whole national in-service budget, about £5–6m, should in future be spent on short-term activities.

Professional centres

A network of 'professional centres' covering the country should be set up. Easily accessible, these could be based on colleges and departments of education and expanded teachers' centres.

'Each would have a full-time warden, of at least senior lecturer status, who would be selected by the centre's management committee, approved by the regional body, and paid by the LEA. He would have an independent role and his chief responsibility would be to draw on all available sources to meet the training requirements of the teachers served by his centre. He would be supported by some full-time staff and by a panel of part-time tutors, drawn from experienced teachers in schools and FE colleges as well as from colleges and university lecturers and LEA advisers.'

Professional centres would cover most of the day-to-day needs of the schools they served and often would house, or arrange, more substantial courses. Once again, this time in a government report, the powerful neutral role of the teachers' centre was identified and praised. Professional centres, said James, should give teachers 'both the means of sharing experience and a point of reference independent of schools and their employers'.

The young teacher, victim of incompetence

If this had been a report on the training of pilots or pharmaceutical products, there would have been a national uproar. For the James Committee harshly criticised the 'gross inadequacy' of existing arrangements for helping new teachers in the schools. They had found 'incompetence and irresponsibility' going on unchecked.

'The probationary teacher, in fact, leaves his college on the last day of term and never hears of or from it again. Nor does the school to which he goes communicate with the college, even if difficulties arrive. He is pleasantly received at his school as would be any newly appointed member of staff, whether or not in a first appointment, and introduced formally or informally to the ways of the place. No one suggests that he is in a special situation or entitled to unusual help. He may be invited by the LEA to attend a tea party but he will probably not go, and, if he does, that will be his last meeting with its officers or advisers. He teaches a full timetable including one or two of the notoriously difficult groups of pupils. No one goes near him in the mistaken belief that to do so would be to interfere with his professional integrity. At the end of the year he receives a note informing him that the probationary year has been satisfactorily completed and he is now a fully qualified teacher.' The gap between theory and practice, declared the report, was alarming.

The James Committee took the view that in any case certain aspects of training could only be given after a young teacher had gained further experience and personal maturity. The myth that fully-fledged teachers emerged from the colleges was at last punctured. Each new teacher, said the report, should be assigned to a specific professional centre, and released for induction activities, for not less than one day a week in the first year – or its residential equivalent in widely dispersed rural areas. A 'professional tutor' should be designated and trained for each school and FE college. He would have special responsibility for the in-service education of the staff, and would consult with his professional centre in working out with each new teacher a programme of studies for the initial year.

Finally, the report urged that certain immediate steps be taken, while recognising that many of its recommendations would have to wait until local government reorganisation was completed in 1974:

1) An interim National Council should be set up.
2) Teachers entering the schools from 1973 should have an improved induction programme. LEA's should therefore start to train professional tutors.
3) Education authorities should continue the expansion of in-service education, making plans, for instance, to develop existing teachers' centres into full professional centres.

Increased activity reported

The educational world bit its nails and speculated exegetically about what decisions Mrs Thatcher would make for implementing the James Report. Almost a year later, the White Paper *Education: A Framework for Expansion* would be issued, in December 1972. A full account of the professional debate which intervened would now be only of historical interest. There was general approval, however, for the expansion of in-service education proposed by the James Committee. Everyone was in favour, too, of improved schemes of induction support for young teachers – but the James proposals for initial training came under heavy fire. No one liked them. The inspectors and organisers, for instance, feared complaints from parents about their children being taught four days a week by unqualified teachers.[7]

The Inner London Education Authority, in its observations on the James Report, approved the expansionary proposals made by the Committee.[8] It was intended in inner London to build up some major professional centres, and despite the difficulties of staffing release, ILEA expected that in-service education would in due course become compulsory. By 1972 ILEA had embarked on an ambitious programme of longer full-time courses, usually of six weeks' duration. There were 34 teachers' centres flourishing in inner London. A new weekly colour magazine, *Contact*, given free to each London teacher, devoted its early issues to profiling them.

How the rise of teachers' centres coincided with an educational technology boom in the schools has already been recorded in discussion of their origins. Early on, a sophisticated collection of audio-visual apparatus in a workshop room often provided the only visual clue to what a teachers' centre was all about. In inner London by 1971, media resources officers, specially trained in information retrieval, closed-circuit television, photography, graphics, reprographics, and sound-recording techniques, were being appointed to teachers' centres. There they were able to build up local resource collections and loan services, undertake creative assignments and advisory visits to schools, run in-service courses and support curriculum development activity. A large Media Resources Centre, serving the whole of inner London, opened in 1972, where teachers were able to preview audio-visual aids, and where subsidised teaching materials were mass-produced by a publishing unit.

Other progressive authorities all over the country were similarly active. It was not surprising to find the effervescent director of the Springbank Centre at Leeds writing in the *Teachers' World*, that in the two years since his last account, the Centre had outgrown its premises.[9] Leeds teachers now wanted an accessible, purpose-built centre in the city centre, providing school library and museum services. At Wigan, the teachers' centre had collaborated with the Open University in opening two seminar rooms on the premises. Audio-visual aids equipment for use by Open University students had been installed and a technician appointed.[10]

The NUT survey of teachers' centres

Intensive coverage was given by the educational press to a survey of teachers' centres, published by the National Union of Teachers early in 1972.[11] Returns were received from only 35% of all centres. This poor response rate no doubt reflected the disenchantment felt by many wardens at the lack of interest shown in their work by the professional associations. Nevertheless, fascinating and clear-cut evidence was presented of superior standards of staffing and equipment at urban compared with rural teachers' centres.

Teachers' centres in the countryside were staffed by fewer

wardens, and more thinly spread with less accommodation and equipment. Three-quarters of the teachers' centres by 1971 were accommodated in separate buildings, especially in the cities, although there was some tendency for specialist centres to be located in schools. Urban teachers' centres had an average of seven rooms available for use, but rural centres only three rooms. Similarly, more money was spent on display and reprographics in the urban centres.

Conditions of employment varied widely. Two-thirds of all wardens were paid as teachers on the Burnham salary scales, but the remainder were paid on a confused mixture of college of education, inspectorate and administrative scales. In 22 centres the leaders were paid only an honorarium and the survey also revealed that four teachers' centres actually charged teachers for attendance at courses!

Activities at half of the centres were controlled by a constitution, involving a joint managing committee on which teachers were represented, or an advisory committee where the teacher's voice was at least heard. A minority of centres housed the advisory team. Teachers' centres often had other assistant staff, usually secretaries and caretakers, although only thirteen centres had appointed a deputy warden. Centre provision ranged from hill-billy frugality to palatial splendour. One large teachers' centre employed a host of estate workers, gardeners, cooks, cleaners and clerical staff – as well as five barmen and fifteen waitresses!

Most wardens visited schools and got a car allowance for doing so. When asked to state in order of importance their main responsibilities, they listed:

1 Administration of courses
2 Organisation of curriculum development
3 Arranging exhibitions
4 Development of resources
5 Visiting schools
6 Servicing study groups
7 Arranging conferences
8 Administration of teacher-groups
9 Liaison with higher education centres
10 Co-operation with the county authority
11 Schools Council projects
12 Social activities

In general, wardens worked between forty and fifty hours per week. The NUT survey concluded that, while professional opinion varied among wardens on the future of teachers' centres, there was unanimity that salaries were derisory, an insult, and completely inappropriate.

The debate in print

By 1972, there was a steady flow of articles and correspondence in journals about teachers' centres. In a letter to *Education*, an irate correspondent complained that teachers' centres had in his view been a waste of money and resources.[12] He thought that the committee set up in 1969 under Sir Lionel Russell to review the whole field might well recommend that the in-service training of teachers, and therefore teachers' centres, should be incorporated into the adult education structure. Another critic, a Warwickshire teacher, argued thoughtfully in *Trends in Education*, that teachers' centres were failing to undertake local curriculum development work.[13] Many overworked teachers, thinking it could be easily undertaken and provided a quick return, had found it was just another burden. Curriculum development needed to be properly timetabled into the school's programme. More was needed than half an hour in the lunch-time, with interruptions from children with bloody knees or messages from Mum. Vigorous local autonomy could only be promoted if local authorities were prepared to pay the cost. Similar regrets were expressed by Jack Walton in *Forum*.[14] In examining the spectacularly rapid rise of centres, he had found them often existing on a financial shoe-string. With certain notable exceptions, such as the centres in the North-West Project, they were not undertaking a dynamic role. Secondary teachers tended to avoid teachers' centres and identification with their low-status primary colleagues. Many LEA's were hesitant about encouraging an organisation run by teachers. So centres had tended to be concerned with low-level 'bread and butter' in-service courses. However, there were grounds for optimism. The teachers' centre was the most economic base for a resource centre. The James Report had prescribed an expanded role for teachers' centres which would move them in the direction of more professionalism, thereby improving the training, status and promotion prospects of wardens.

J. G. Owen, now the Devon County Education Officer, looked at the current situation in the teachers' centres in 1972.[15] What determined the success or failure of a centre? A centre linked with a national project had, he thought, the best chance of survival. Other centres succeeded through strong leadership or because the local advisers, college of education or university staff supported them. In the city, teachers' centres had sometimes been ineffective when faced with the teaching problems of a decayed urban area where the whole community was anti-educational. Sometimes a city teacher had no energy left for the task of professional self-renewal. In the country, ice on the roads or a large lawn in need of mowing could discourage teachers from travelling to the centre. Sometimes a teacher had become so accustomed to isolation that he was put off by the strangeness of meeting other teachers to examine professional problems. There was something special about teachers' centres, however. Although they were barely seven years old, they had been a highly successful strategy. In Britain's loose educational structure they were a nodal point at which pressures could meet. The ensuing clash might be conflict or co-operation, this would vary. But the invention of teachers' centres and local teacher-based reform was going to have far-reaching effects not only in Britain but also on the educational systems of other developed countries. Ronald Cave, in a book about curriculum development, recorded a similar verdict.[16]

Research into teachers' centres

By the end of 1972 a number of individual researches had looked at teachers' centres. Studies of the role of the teachers' centre warden in relation to a sixth form general studies course,[17] attitudes of teachers towards the Huntingdon teachers' centre,[18] an enquiry into several teachers' centres during a period of educational change,[19] and a one-man national survey,[20] had all been undertaken.

At Nottingham, J. Brand, himself a warden, investigated how wardens and others saw teachers' centres.[21] His general findings were familiar. He recommended that teachers' centres should go on the road like mobile libraries with their courses. More administrative help was needed for wardens so that they could visit secondary schools and encourage the staffs there to join in centre activities. There should be a major increase in day-time courses at teachers' centres, asserted Brand, and staffing ratios needed adjustment so that large urban or small rural schools could release teachers with equal ease.

The videotape recorder has been described as 'the greatest thing for kids since the invention of sliced bread'. It was not surprising therefore to find a teacher being financed by the Independent Television Authority to make a special study of the potential use of the videotape recorder for in-service education.[22] J. T. Pound reported in 1972 that five Welsh teachers' centres had co-operated in showing videotapes about 'the open-plan school' to discussion groups of teachers. All of the teachers were enthusiastic about the use of television for in-service education. But the poverty of teachers' centre provision in rural areas was rammed home. The ITA school-teacher fellow had not found a single teachers' centre in Wales in 1971 which possessed a videotape recorder.

The most important small research to date was conducted by E. J. Hollick, who looked at the in-service training of primary teachers in the Hampshire and Kent teachers' centres.[23] There was such demand for short courses at the teachers' centres in these two counties in 1971, he found, that 35% of the teachers were failing to obtain a place.

A key to this remarkable success story seemed to be the extent to which the centres were recruiting classroom teachers to run their courses. (It will be remembered that the DES 1967 survey showed only 4% of teachers had been involved in staffing courses in the three previous years.) In Hampshire 48% and in Kent 42% of all teachers' centre courses in 1971 were staffed by serving teachers. Even then, Hollick found, a pool of talent still remained. Teachers and head teachers were convinced that at least one member of each school staff would make a good course leader for part of the teachers' centre programme. No machinery, however, existed to make sure this happened. Teachers were diffident about putting themselves forward. A talent-spotter was needed, someone in authority who could pick out potential lecturers and workshop leaders from among classroom teachers. My own experiences confirm Hollick's findings. In West London we have placed unusual emphasis on courses run by the practising classroom teacher. Teachers working in Hammersmith, Kensington and Chelsea schools staff 60% of the Sherbrooke Centre courses, 20% are led by other ILEA teachers, and the remaining 20% are staffed by distinguished outside lecturers such as Professor Geoffrey Matthews.

Hollick, like Brand, concluded that teachers' centres needed to travel out to the consumer. Popular courses should be put on circuit, using annexes to teachers' centres and school buildings in the evening. These recommendations also bear out the experience of most wardens of centres. For instance, in an educational district which extends five miles from Kensal Rise cemetery to Putney Bridge, having some of the worst traffic congestion in Western Europe, we have found it advisable to locate half of all the courses in accessible schools. When teachers do travel from their schools to local centres in inner London, the education authority pays their often substantial travel expenses.

The White Paper

In late 1972 the editor of *The Times Higher Educational Supplement* revealed that several radical initiatives in British educational policy would be announced in a White Paper to be published shortly.[24] They would represent the biggest shift in priorities since 1944.

These predictions proved accurate. In her White Paper, *Education: A Framework for Expansion,* Mrs Margaret Thatcher covered matters ranging from nursery education to university finance.[25] The White Paper disagreed with the James Report over the initial training of teachers. Instead it proposed a new three-year course of teacher-training incorporating educational studies and leading to a B.Ed. degree and qualified status. The White Paper agreed emphatically with the James Committee that young teachers needed special help and support. One-fifth of their time should therefore be set aside for in-service education in the first year. They should also have a lightened timetable for the rest of the week, so that each new teacher would only undertake three-quarters of a full teaching load.

Professional tutors would need to be designated and trained through a network of professional centres, based on existing training institutes and teachers' centres. The government proposed to set up pilot schemes of induction in 1973/74, in areas not heavily affected by local government reorganisation, when new arrangements for helping teachers in their first year could be tried out. A national programme would be introduced in all the schools in 1975/76.

Experienced teachers should be released for in-service education, said the White Paper, for the equivalent of one term in every seven years. The in-service programme should strike a careful balance between the teachers' personal interest in his professional development and the employer's concern with the current needs of particular schools and the pupils in them. A target of 3% or release of teachers would be aimed for by 1981.

The area training organisations based on the universities, who had been responsible since 1948 for co-ordinating and supervising teacher education, were to be replaced by new machinery. The 160 colleges of education were to change their role. They would in future train fewer teachers, sharing instead in the expansion of higher education and in the growth of in-service education and professional centres for teachers. Some colleges might even close. The massive expansion of in-service training and induction support would cost £55m by 1981, compared with the 1971/72 budget of £6m.

Mrs Thatcher concluded that, after consultation with the teaching profession, she might decide to create a Teaching Council along the lines suggested by the James Report. In the meantime the government would look for vigorous preparation for the expansion to come.

1. Sandilands, A., *A Place to Pool Ideas,* Teacher, Vol. 17, No. 23, 4 June 1971, p. 3.
2. Stevens, Auriol, *Centres for Action,* Times Educational Supplement, No. 2592, 17 December 1971, p. 14.
3. *The Teachers' Centre Concept,* Trends in Education, July 1971, pp. 42–7.
   (1) Arnold, R., *A Centre in Britain* (Newham)
   (2) Boucher, Leon, *A Centre in Maryland, U.S.A.*
4. Williams, Louis, *The Next Step,* Teacher in Wales, Vol. II, No. 5, 23 April 1971, pp. 10–11.
5. *National Conference for Wardens of Teachers' Centres,* First Report University of London Institute of Education. Distributed for WISE, 1971.
6. *Teacher Education and Training (James Report),* H.M.S.O., 1972.
7. *'James Report' Inspectors' doubts on Licensed Year,* Education, 18 August 1972, p. 120.
8. *Teacher Training and Education,* ILEA, Education Sub-Committee Report, 12 July 1972.
9. *Spring Bank Teachers' Centre, Leeds,* Teachers' World, 26 May 1972, p. 22.
10. Crawford, K., *Wigan Teachers' Centre,* Education, 21 April 1972, p. 379.
11. *Teachers' Centres.* A Survey of Centre Resources and conditions of service of Leaders, NUT, March 1972.
12. Letters to the Editor, Education, 1 September 1972, p. 163.
13. Richards, Colin, *Teachers' Centres – A Primary School View,* Trends in Education, No. 25, January 1972, pp. 31–33.
14. Walton, J., *Teachers' Centres: Their Role and Function,* Forum, Autumn 1972.
15. Owen, J. G., *Developing Teachers' Centres,* Trends in Education, No. 28, October 1972, pp. 2–7.

16. Cave, Ronald G., *An Introduction to Curriculum Development*, Ward Lock, 1971, p. 21.
17. Spackman, R. C., A Consideration of the role of the Teachers' Centre Warden as an external change agent with reference to sixth form general studies project. Unpublished. M.Ed. Thesis University of Bristol School of Education, 1972.
18. Bennett, J., Huntingdon Teachers' Centre and the Attitudes of Teachers towards this Teachers' Centre. Unpublished. Dip.Ed. Dissertation, University of Nottingham, 1970.
19. Roff, W. D., Teachers' Centres: A Study of Teachers' Centres and their function during a period of Educational Change. Unpublished. Dissertation, Cambridge Institute of Education, 1971.
20. Garland, R. G., Aspects of the Development Function and Structure of the English Teachers' Centre. Unpublished Thesis, University of Lancaster, 1972.
21. Brand, J. H. B., The In-service Education role of the Teachers' Centre. Unpublished M.Phil. Thesis, University of Nottingham, 1972.
22. Pound, J. T., An enquiry into the possible uses of Educational Television as one medium for the in-service training of teachers in Teachers' Centres, University College of South Wales and Monmouthshire Department of Education, 1971, mimeographed.
23. Hollick, E. G., A study of the In-service Training of Primary School teachers with particular reference to teacher contribution and teachers' centres. Unpublished special study. Diploma of Child Development, University of London Institute of Education, 1972.
24. *Mrs. Thatcher backs James in-service plan but cuts back university graduate courses*, Times Higher Educational Supplement, No. 56, 10 November 1972, p. 1.
25. *Education: A Framework for Expansion* (White Paper), H.M.S.O., December 1972.

4 *A Beginning of Teachers' Centres*

GEOFFREY MATTHEWS

IT DEPENDS WHAT YOU MEAN BY A TEACHERS' CENTRE. A GOOD working definition is a meeting-place for at least two people concerned with learning. The first teachers' centre was accordingly the Garden of Eden, and the first course (on experimental pomology) was an open-ended voyage of discovery for the participants without even the blessing of Higher Authority. Since then, there have been many varieties of teachers' centres, providing between them recreational facilities, lectures, residential and other courses, opportunities for teachers to discuss recent development (notably in science teaching) among themselves. There is, however, a particular brand of teachers' centre whose main purpose is to demonstrate the intimate connection between curriculum development and teacher education (the latter often known bleakly as 'in-service training'). The Nuffield Mathematics Project was concerned with setting up the prototypes for this sort of centre, in circumstances which will now be described.

The Nuffield Mathematics Project

Mathematics has long been a notorious subject. Efforts to make the man in the street more numerate (a fashionable if ill-defined word) have been baulked by his memories of parroted tables and unlikely commands such as 'turn it upside down and multiply' or 'add a nought'. The launching of the first Russian Sputnik in 1957 provided an impetus for the reappraisal of the subject, and by 1961 a number of secondary teachers were taking a hard look at the New Maths. As a result a number of projects were started and in due course text-books started to appear. The Nuffield Foundation had meantime made a substantial investment in science and as this was clearly going to be successful they approached the Ministry to see if something also needed doing for mathematics. The answer came that the 'private army' projects had already moved in at secondary level but that the primary field was wide open and indeed the time was ripe for development: the beginning of the end of the 11-plus was leaving teachers with the feeling that much of the old stuff was obsolete and unintelligible and that here was an opportunity to teach something more relevant and palatable – but what?

In August 1963 I was handed a slip of paper by Tony Becher, Assistant Director (Education) of the Nuffield Foundation and he asked if I was interested. The paper mentioned quite shortly the possibility of a project for a 'contemporary course in mathematics for children aged 8–13'. The idea of going up to 13, and so overlapping the first two secondary years, seemed excellent, as clearly there would be a need for any 'primary' project to take account of the new secondary developments. But starting at 8? I heard myself saying 'I don't believe you can start at 8. The damage may well have been done by that time – if we could start at 5, I'd like the job.' To my astonishment Tony Becher pulled out his pen and changed the '8' into a '5' on the spot, and there could be no retreat.

The project was not to start till September 1964, so there was plenty of time to gather a writing team and plan strategy. A first and obvious need was an office, and as the Foundation had no accommodation available at that time I was invited to look round on my own account. A desperate search ended when I was looking one day through the replies from local authorities to a circular sent out by the British Association. I forget what information had been requested by the committee concerned, but certainly among the answers there was one which struck me as particularly helpful and friendly, from Mr Ron Openshaw, Chief Education Officer of Newham. He accepted an invitation to lunch at Leoni's: over sherry he'd see what he could do, the hors d'œuvres brought the offer of a couple of rooms at New City School, Newham; by coffee the whole top floor was available, with temporary secretarial help, if required, and, the bill settled, we set off to inspect the site together. Shortly afterwards, the Foundation discovered some office accommodation in Central London, but the top floor of New City was by this time firmly earmarked for the Project and in fact became the first operational teachers' centre.

Pilot areas

The plan was to have a dozen 'pilot areas' for the Project, which would try out our draft materials and produce feedback in return for free copies and such spearhead courses as we could run with a small team whose main commitment was planning, writing and observing how our ideas were being received. A letter was sent to all the local authorities in England and Wales (the first of a string starting 'Dear Chief Education Officer') and 100 of them replied that they would be most disappointed if they weren't chosen. It was therefore necessary to send a second letter with fiercer conditions; each authority would have to choose an area involving about 100 teachers (infant, junior and secondary), be responsible for all their own training beyond the spearhead courses, and set up a centre with someone in charge who would co-ordinate and ensure a good flow of constructive criticism of the 'Teachers' Guides'. A dozen authorities dropped out at this stage but it was still a very difficult task choosing pilots with a good spread (rural/urban, prosperous, deprived, etc.), at the same time causing as little offence as possible. To make matters worse there was heavy pressure from Scotland, who forcefully wanted to know why they'd been left out and rightly so, as eventually they produced some of the finest feed-back. The pilot areas chosen, after much sorting and re-sorting, were

Birmingham (Moseley / King's Heath)
Bristol (Withywood, Brislington)
Cambridgeshire (City and neighbouring rural area)
Cardiff (Llanrumney Estate)
Doncaster (Urban)
Edinburgh (Rosebank)
Hampshire (Winchester)
ILEA (Ladbroke, North Kensington)
Kent (Folkestone)
Middlesbrough (Eastern outskirts)
Newham (inevitably centred on New City School)
Northumberland (Whitley Bay)
Somerset (Yeovil)
Staffordshire (Kidsgrove)

Each area had a teachers' centre as focal point; 7 of these were in flourishing schools, 1 in a hut behind a school, 2 in disused schools, 1 in a technical college and 3 in separate buildings (one of these being a disused aerodrome). There were of course teething troubles. One area decided at first to dispense with a warden, and two devoted teachers nearly worked themselves into the ground keeping the place going in their 'spare time'; the aerodrome was a strange centre – miles from any of the contributing schools (it was replaced as soon as possible by a splendid house at the heart of things); one authority was so large that the Centre got lost for a year in a maze of administrative machinery (but when it was finally opened it was one of the most efficient and best-equipped). And one authority made the mistake of designating a conveniently clustered collection of schools as the 'Nuffield Pilot Area' without proper consultation with the teachers. My initial meeting there, ostensibly for me to explain what they'd let themselves in for, turned out as an occasion for airing many grievances and ended with the surprising question 'Is it true that Mrs —— has inside toilets, and if so, why has she one more infant helper than I have?'

But all these difficulties passed quickly. The 'Area Organiser', whom we'd stipulated as chief correspondent with Project HQ, was usually a very sympathetic member of the authority's staff and occasionally the warden of the centre himself. The vital point was that the centre should be seen to be run by and for the teachers; one of the most successful centres seemed to have every teacher for miles around on the committee.

Second-phase areas

It must be explained that the number of centres did not long remain at 14. Some of the authorities which had not been chosen for pilot areas were quite furious, and the Project found itself under pressure from the newly-established Schools Council to extend its trials. At the time it seemed highly dangerous to disperse our first draft guides more widely, as some at least were very experimental and would clearly need a good deal of re-writing before they were finally passed for publication. On the other hand it seemed a great pity not to cash in on the wave of enthusiasm which undoubtedly was sweeping the country. Accordingly, with some misgivings, we admitted 77 'Second-Phase Areas'. These were in fresh LEA's, each again to have a group of trial schools services by a teachers' centre. The second-phase areas had copies of the trial guides, at cost price, and more feed-back began to come in. Eventually 44 'continuation areas' joined, buying the final editions as they came on to the market, so that by this time there were only a handful of LEA's who weren't involved in some way. The project grew according to the 'window principle' – one teacher would experiment, another would look in through the window and want to get started too; a group of teachers from one school would spread the message to others via the teachers' centres, and so on. Within an LEA with a pilot area, other areas would be opened up (at an early stage in Northumberland I asked to go to the teachers' centre and was asked 'Which one?' There were four of them by that time). Pilots would also spread the message to second-phase areas, and so on.

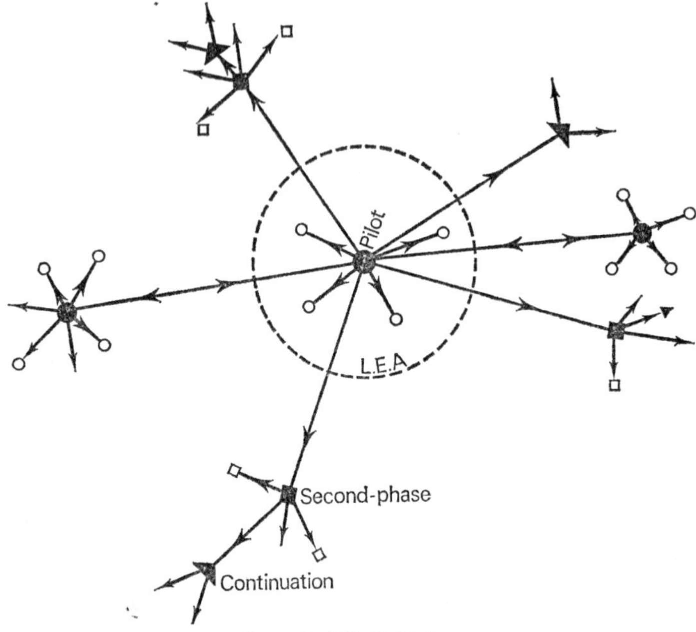

Spread of Nuffield Areas

The teachers' centre

In the British manner, no two teachers' centres have looked alike or been organised in the same way. All the same each of the centres contains three main elements:

(1) *A working room*
Here teachers can try out materials and make their own.

(2) *A discussion room*
This probably includes the library and is comfortably furnished so that teachers can exchange problems and ideas in a relaxed atmosphere.

(3) *A refreshment area*
This varies from a pantry to a cafeteria, but in any case the focal point of every centre is the tea urn. Without this, there would certainly be no teachers, and so no centre. There are also, of course, toilet facilities and various op-

tional extras – for example at Stapleford, which serves a large area of Cambridgeshire, there is a kitchen where teachers can prepare their own snacks.

The work of a centre includes the following:

(1) Meetings to discuss the Nuffield publications and how they went down in the classrooms; courses as the need arises (these activities will be considered in more detail later).
(2) Meetings 'for at least two people concerned with learning'. Even the most attractively produced Guide is difficult to read on one's own, but with someone else there it can be fun (or at least there is a shoulder to cry on). Young teachers especially find it useful to know that they have similar problems; examples of children's work can be brought in for discussion ('I wish I'd thought of that').
(3) Making apparatus. On an early visit to Whitley Bay I was approached by three ladies in as many minutes. Each complained privately that she was nearing exhaustion trying to produce written assignments for the children. I introduced them to each other and they formed a team, swopping ideas and even cards, and then finding they could cope.

Apparatus has a wide definition. On one visit to the Hannah More Centre at Bristol, I found the whole place filled with home-made rabbit hutches. This was one of four centres shared with the Nuffield Junior Science Project, and the teachers had decided to go in for mass production.

The centres are part of the whole in-service network. Apart from the spearhead courses mentioned earlier (lasting up to a fortnight), there are longer courses, for example at Colleges of Education, lasting a term or even a year. The aim is to have at least one person in each primary school who is thoroughly on the mathematical hook and to whom the rest of the staff can turn for advice. But as many as possible should keep up to date by regular visits to the local centre.

The original purpose of providing Nuffield feed-back has by now largely been fulfilled. This was the central feature of the project, the teachers really being involved in the production of the materials. Three Guides were very largely rewritten as the result of the friendly but tough criticism and another, on *Space*, which I thought was excellent, was literally destroyed because the pilot areas didn't accept it. In this way, at least, the point was well made that 'they listen to us', though happily 'we and they' has not been a feature of the project.

The writing team indeed became heavily involved in the local work. Each member would spend about half his time devising materials and the other half finding out what the teachers, and children, thought of them. We have all spent many hours crawling about on classroom floors talking to children and indeed some of the best feed-back has come from a diffident teacher in her own surroundings ('I didn't like to say it in front of the others, but I don't really understand that bit on page 6').

Sometimes the team would descend *en masse* on a pilot area and spend the inside of a week visiting schools and meeting people at the centre. The 'team' really was a team in every sense – not forgetting the secretaries, from Julie Shaw to Lynda Thompson, who have taken everything in their stride from the typing and retyping of innumerable manuscripts to soothing important but totally unexpected visitors from abroad and putting up with the pleasantries and eccentricities of the writers. An early memory is the sight of Julie's beautiful patent-leather shoes gradually sinking into the sands of Redcar as she listened to an impromptu address on Shape and Size by George Corston. Not even this ruffled her, and nothing would stop the team from talking shop at every opportunity.

These pioneering days are over, but there will always be much local work to be done. Fresh teachers arrive, and the scheme of work must be constantly scrutinised so that it doesn't fossilise the way it did during the previous 75 years. (There would have been no need for a Nuffield Project if a lively network of teachers' centres had been set up much earlier.) It is most encouraging the number of areas which have devised their own schemes ('The Southampton Guide to the

Nuffield Guides', etc.) to supplement the nationally produced materials; other areas, equally well, have decided that the local development can be continued less formally, with meetings and discussions.

Just as teachers can feel lonely (and perhaps the most important effect of the project has been the opening of windows and doors – between classrooms), so can organisers and leaders. There have therefore been a series of annual conferences for these key people, 'Scraptofts', named after the Leicester College where they were first held.

Courses and meetings

The first Nuffield course to be held at a teachers' centre was, of course, at New City School, Newham. As an introduction, the teachers were plunged into practical work. The theory could come later, the all-important start was to break down the barriers of fear which surrounded mathematics. The scene was set carefully, with plenty of attractive 'apparatus' and enticing starting points, but in spite of all these precautions, there was soon trouble. Walking across the hall from one room to another I became aware of a commotion, shouts of 'Is there a doctor in the house?' and the school-keeper saying, as helpfully as possible, 'Well, that's Dr Matthews over there.' And so I became involved in my first (and I hope last) medical case; happily, I was able to produce a rapid and complete cure. The charming young lady who was brought to me for treatment was really in quite a bad way. She was not only crying her eyes out but also shaking and visibly getting more and more upset. Eventually she managed to sob out her trouble: 'That man I was working with – he said "Isn't it fun working in the geometry room?"' Suddenly the poor girl had been taken back to her own school-days, when the theorems and definitions had apparently literally been beaten into her, and the very thought of going back to 'geometry' was too much. 'The man's a fool,' I replied, 'it's not the geometry room' (how do I get out of this one?) – 'it's the shape and size room.' And she cheered up and went back to work on the problem of tessellations of the shapes she and her colleague had cut out. The Nuffield Project Guides on geometry to this day are all labelled 'Shape and Size'.

This story illustrates the extreme care which is needed in running a course. The teachers want to start with reassurance and from their existing base, with reasonably quick pay-off for their own classroom. At one of the early 'spearhead' courses, the team lost the members completely by introducing a session on groups. Although this was light-hearted and apparently painless, it was a question of 'What's he to Hecuba, or Hecuba to him?'

A worse experience happened at one of the second-phase centres. A roomful of teachers, normally cheerful and active, looked hot, tired and resentful when I arrived and at last someone plucked up courage and asked me, 'What's the difference between equality and equivalence?' I replied that I had no idea and didn't really think it mattered a lot, and everyone was beaming again. Someone had evidently been addressing them for an hour on this topic.

Much of the most valuable work at the centre arises spontaneously – a group of teachers is worried about the teaching of some topic, the question arises of how to keep records, and so on; a study group is then well motivated and may even ask someone in to lecture to them. But there is certainly a place for short courses, say half a dozen weekly sessions on a topic. It is difficult to time these to everyone's satisfaction. One compromise is 'half our time, half yours', say a session from 3 to 5 p.m., but many teachers prefer soon after school say 4.30 to 6.30, while in other areas (notably urban ones with travel difficulties) courses have been run from 2 to 4 or 4.30. This is a matter of course for local negotiation. In principle it seems reasonable to follow the James Report and White Paper to the extent of providing more in-service courses in school time.

An inoculation course

The following is a pattern for an 'inoculation course', for teachers who are either new to primary mathematics teaching or who have hitherto been forced to slog through '11-plus maths', with its 'timeses' and 'gozintas' (the problem of how one number 'goes into' another, i.e. division).

Session 1 Vital statistics

The teachers are split up into groups of 6 to 10. Each group chooses *one* property such as shoe size, birth month, favourite colour, distance travelled from home to school, etc. etc. Information is collected from everyone in turn and the group then has to present this in say 6 ways, at least 2 of which are 3-dimensional. There is an assortment of pens, paper and material round the room (see below). This exercise has much to commend it:

(a) There is some real mathematics to be conjured out of the environment without too much effort. The teachers are told during the session that they must accompany their work with some written conclusions.
(b) It is fun. Everyone gets on first-name terms.
(c) It shows the possibility of group work.
(d) It takes a long time (up to 2 hours), the teachers are busily noisy and they are not often sitting down. There are several morals here for the classroom.

Session 2 'Old' is not 'Bad'

This session gives a reassurance that everything we ever did previously was not wrong. But it could question, for example, *why* we 'do' a sum like 53×29 and what skills the children need to be able to invent a method for doing it instead of listening to teacher's famous rule of 'add a nought'. The philosophy is twofold:

Children are different
Young children learn by doing.[1]

Session 3 Junk and Sets

The teachers have been asked to bring 'kitchen-sink' materials with them, and there is a discussion of the mathematics which can be derived from these. The word 'set' is de-bunked; some new writers have shrouded it in mystery, but it is simply at the heart of mathematics learning. Children do not learn about 3 before they have seen many sets of three objects, 3 spoons, 3 forks, 3 pencils, 3 biscuits, etc. etc.

Section 4 Structural apparatus

There are a number of kits on the market, Cuisenaire rods, Dienes Multi-base Arithmetic blocks, Logiblocks etc. Teachers should see these and explore their possibilities by actually handling them but, just as importantly, should realise their limitations. Mathematics is abstracted from a wide variety of experiences, in which these 'bought' kits may have a place.

Session 5 Checking Up and Records

How do we know just where the children are in their thinking? Some guidance has been given by a joint venture of the Nuffield Project and Piaget's team at Geneva.[2]

Sessions 6, 7 Into Action

Discussion of methods of working including construction of assignments and other materials. Introduction to the Nuffield Guides.

All this is of course, only a start. The course will have been a success if there are a series of follow-up meetings, the teachers gradually becoming absorbed in the activities of the centre.

Films can play an important part. Five of these, made as a joint BBC/Nuffield effort, have had an enormous effect. These form the series 'Children and Mathematics' and consist of:

1. We still need arithmetic
2. Common sense and New Maths
3. Let the children think
4. Checking up
5. Teachers at the centre

The first four can very profitably be used with the inoculation course; the fifth is a description of the growth and purpose of teachers' centres. The Nuffield Project has made three other films which centres have found useful:

Mathematics with everything (Infants)
I do and I understand (Juniors)
Into Secondary School[3]

Other courses and events

Other courses will suggest themselves: Probability and Statistics, topics from 'Shapes and Size' and from 'Computation and Structure', Computing, Recording and so on.

Progression is essential; a few ideas picked up from the 'inoculation course' won't serve well if dished up at random to children of all ages. There is grave danger in the Trundling Syndrome – long-suffering children with the clicking wheel, purposelessly measuring the playground for years and years and years. Mercifully, there is a very definite progression, and this is reflected in the Nuffield Guides.

It must, however, again be emphasised that courses are no substitute for the informal meetings which form the basis of the work at the teachers' centre.

Resources

For a course like the 'inoculation' one described above, there must be a good deal of equipment, for example:

Paper of different sizes and colours
Cardboard sheets
Various types of graph paper
Miscellaneous coloured pencils, felt pens
Wooden building cubes (assorted colours)
String (assorted colours)
Ribbon
Plasticine
Threading beads
Popper beads
Scissors
Sellotape

Miscellaneous containers
Scales
Self-locking cubes (e.g. Unifix)
Sand
Pebbles
Marbles
Balls and cylinders
Tape measures
Coloured gummed paper
Cardboard boxes

There will also be a library and a film projector, and probably other AVA equipment (tapes, loops) and reprographic materials, especially useful for teachers from small schools without duplicating facilities.

The centre will also have a collection of the various commercial apparatus, for teachers to try out and assess for themselves. Sometimes equipment manufacturers are allowed to set up a temporary exhibition of their wares. This may save teachers valuable travelling time and is certainly more effective than simply using catalogues, but the teachers must exercise discrimination – exhibition of equipment at the centre does not necessarily imply that it is of any use.

Multi-purpose centres

After the centres had been going for a year or so, people started whispering, e.g., 'Dr Matthews, I hope you don't mind, we had a French session in your centre last night.' An even more surprising comment was made by James Shanks, Her Majesty's Chief Inspector (Primary Schools) for Scotland. His greeting was 'To hell with mathematics.' When I understood his meaning, I could only agree with him; he went on to explain that he saw the Nuffield Mathematics Project as a lever for introducing a new attitude into the whole curriculum. Indeed it would be very difficult (and foolish) to keep mathematics separate from everything else. It was, therefore, highly desirable that there should be opportunities at the same centre to discuss the children as a whole and not in terms of subject segments (one of my team declined a request to define the place of New Maths in one sentence, but said she could do for the traditional arithmetic: 'The place of Arithmetic is between Scripture and Milk'). Gradually over half the mathematics centres changed their names to teachers' centres, while others grew up from the beginning as 'multi-purpose'. An example is Sherbrooke, where Robert Thornbury is the warden, and where I have shared the building with every sort of activity and incidentally run my first course for nursery teachers. One great strength of the centres is the ability to attract teachers of children over the whole span of schooling, and some of the most profitable sessions have included infant, junior and secondary teachers getting together and sharing experiences and difficulties.

Wardens

Just as a school is as good as its staff, so a teachers' centre is as good as its warden. (It's not a question of the building – some of the best centres have been in tumbledown, even condemned quarters.) Most of the wardens are first-class, dedicated people, but there are many pitfalls and temptations. Some of these are illustrated by the following 'Warnings for a Young Warden'.

The Seven Deadly Sins

1. *Pride*
   'This is the first of ten talks on Algebraic Structure; of course I'm a mathematician and you are not, and you'll need 80 sessions before you really . . .'
2. *Lust*
   'I'm asking if I can't take over the two neighbouring boroughs . . .'
3. *Envy*
   'I hear that Bloggs has 5 activities going on at his centre on a Tuesday. Very well, I must have 6 – let's see, an extra guitar class at intermediate level should do the trick.'

4. *Wrath*
   'Only 5 people turned up for that course I laid on specially – disgraceful!'
5. *Gluttony*
   'I'll lay on another course on pictorial representation. I know they've had 3 recently, but you can't have enough birthday graphs, eh?'
6. *Avarice*
   'Now we've got closed-circuit television, we must have a second channel, and our own radio station, and . . .'
7. *Sloth*
   'Come in, Dr Matthews. Excuse me a minute, I'm so busy I don't know which way to turn. I'll be with you in a minute. I'm just signing my application to have a deputy warden.'

Of course no one behaves like this, but the temptations are there.

The good warden appears to have all the time in the world, is in fact up to his eyes and spends much of his time with proper humility listening to the requests of teachers – he even visits schools! He can't hope to know all the answers himself (he'd look foolish if he tried), but with diligence he will know where to look and whom to involve.

The future

Teachers' centres are here to stay. The Nuffield areas have grouped themselves together into regions, and national conferences continue without any impetus from HQ. The organisation of the most recent one (Furzedown 1972) was nothing to do with me whatsoever and it was acclaimed as the best yet.

Curriculum development in this country is taking place more slowly than in Scotland (where there is more control) and faster than in the States (where perhaps there is more inertia). Our brand of educational anarchy ensures freedom for those who want to do nothing, and stay in the nineteenth century, as well as for those who have a mind to experiment. But this price for freedom is worth paying; the important thing is that the teacher can think if he wants to. Curriculum Development and Teacher Education become two phrases for the same thing, and our schools can be kept alive by continuous development of the curriculum with local inspiration. The key to this, of course, is the active teachers' centre.

1. For further details, see, for example, *Mathematics Through School,* edited G. Matthews, John Murray, 1972.
2. *Checking Up,* I, II, Chambers and Murray for Nuffield Foundation.
3. For details of hire or purchase, see notes at end of *Mathematics Through School.*

5 *The New Professionals*

HARRY KAHN

SUDDENLY YOU ARE A 'WARDEN'! FROM A CLEARLY DEFINED career as a classroom teacher in primary and secondary schools stretching over a considerable period of your life, at a stroke you are in charge of a teachers' centre. Until recently your daily routine had been well established and you were putting into practice the training which you had received before entering the profession. Now you are in an educational no-man's-land with little help to guide you through its uncharted expanses and only the occasional oasis of another teachers' centre and its warden there to give you succour.

Having come to teaching as a mature student at Borough Road Training College, as it was then called, I spent two years teaching all subjects in primary schools in north-west London before deciding that my knowledge of such topics as 'Who burnt which cakes and when?' was too limited for the needs of a good primary school teacher and that I would be more usefully employed teaching the subject I knew a little about – mathematics – in a secondary school. The next eight years I spent in various types of secondary school – secondary modern, grammar and comprehensive – at first teaching the subject in the traditional manner that had served for so many years. However, at this time the 'modern mathematics' teaching movement was gaining momentum as one of the early forerunners of curriculum development and its message of understanding rather than rote learning was one which could not be ignored. So that, at the time of applying for the post of Warden of the Enfield Teachers' Centre, I was head of the mathematics department in an Enfield comprehensive school which had a modern approach to the teaching of mathematics. What relevance this had to the characteristics of the warden sought by those making the appointment is none too clear! However, at this time, 1968, the whole teachers' centre movement was as yet in its early infancy; and I suspect neither the interviewers nor the candidates for the post had any real idea of the future potential of centres. Certainly all the candidates had gleaned their ideas with which to impress the committee from the only available source at that time – the Schools Council Working Paper No. 10.[1]

This document, which deals with 'Curriculum Development', states that '. . . the Council hopes that in as many areas as possible local education authorities, whether singly or in collaboration with neighbouring authorities, should consider ways of responding to the expressed wish of teachers to come together to conduct for themselves curriculum development . . .' (1.7). The Council also offers '. . . suggestions about those facilities which could best support curriculum development on a local basis . . . such facilities would clearly be of value for other purposes, particularly for in-service training. . . .' While the entire document ran to only some ten pages the new development in English education which it heralded has, since then, expanded to a degree where its influence is felt in almost every classroom in the country. Certainly, in the four and a half years of its existence the Enfield Teachers' Centre has satisfied an obviously unfulfilled need by teachers in the borough and at the same time influenced the pattern of in-service education to the benefit of teachers and pupils alike.

Setting up the Enfield Teachers' Centre

Enfield is one of the 32 Greater London boroughs created in 1965 out of the previous Edmonton, Southgate and Enfield boroughs. It is situated to the north-east of London and is in the main urban, though at its borders with Hertfordshire the environment becomes more rural and there remain one or two of the old 'village' type of schools with one class for infants and one for juniors of all ages. At its western end is the Southgate area which is mainly upper middle class: at the eastern end is Edmonton, a predominantly working-class area with a fairly large concentration of industry; and in the centre is 'old' Enfield which is a mixture of the two. The population of the borough is about 266,000 and it has 32 Infant, 31 Junior, 24 Junior Mixed and Infant, 18 Comprehensive, 1 Grammar and 6 Special Schools. There are some 2,000 teachers employed full-time and 200 part-time in the borough. Comprehensive education was introduced in 1967 by the amalgamation of secondary modern and grammar schools into a comprehensive school system. On the whole, the schools in the west of the borough had built up a well-established grammar school tradition, while in the east good work had been done by secondary modern schools. There is one technical college, one college of technology and one college of education in the borough. The one teachers' centre is a multi-purpose one covering the needs of teachers in all branches of education and in all subjects of the curriculum.

Teachers in the borough are able to express their views on matters related to their work in educating the children of the area through a Joint Consultative Committee which is comprised, in equal parts, of representatives of the Education Committee and the Teachers' Committee. It was the members of this Teachers' Committee, together with the borough's dozen or so advisers, who work under the auspices of the Chief Education Officer to advise teachers on different subjects in the curriculum, who pressed for the establishment of a teachers' centre and eventually convinced the Education Committee of the advantages of the idea. A working party composed of advisers and members of the Teachers' Committee investigated various possible buildings in which space could be made available for a centre before recommending a site. The premises chosen, a bungalow-style building, had become vacant when, with the introduction of comprehensive education, the school which it served as a craft annexe moved to new accommodation. It was selected for a number of reasons – it was accessible by public and private transport from most parts of the borough; it was not a normal type school building and could therefore be easily converted for adult use; the centre would be the sole user of the building; the accommodation in terms of rooms was ideal for a small teachers' centre and it had facilities for car-parking by visiting teachers. Its only real drawback was the fact that the lease would expire in 1970 and its renewal could not be guaranteed. Nevertheless, it was thought that if the centre had become an established educational fact by the date of expiry the chances for renewal would be good, a hope which proved correct. This limited lease of life had immediate effects for good and bad on the conversion of the building to centre usage. Public funds could not be invested in alterations which might have a life span of less than two years. As a result, members of the working party who recommended the use of these premises – advisers, head teachers and teachers – spent considerable periods of time with paints and tools preparing the premises. This initial involvement in the preparation of the very fabric of the building by those for whom the centre would cater set a tradition, continued by the voluntary assistance in alterations from time to time by the craft technician of a local secondary school, which has led to the present maximum use of every corner of the building.

The rooms at the disposal of the centre today are: a lecture room seating up to a maximum of 200, adaptable for exhibitions, small working parties, film projection, etc.; a workshop, to accommodate 30 teachers for practical courses, adaptable for use as an extra lecture room, and with large store cupboards for all types of materials for courses; A library–TV room, with books on modern developments in education, and a wide range of professional journals; a lounge and servery, in which teas and light refreshments (toasted snacks, etc.) are served daily, also used by committees and working parties, social activities and where necessary serving as an additional lecture room; A warden's office, a secretary's office, cloakroom and toilet facilities.

In furnishing the centre care was taken to create an adult atmosphere which would be different to the school environment in which teachers worked all day, enabling them to relax in pleasant surroundings. Prior to the establishment of teachers' centres, in-service teacher education mostly took place in the school classrooms, often using the children's furniture, a situation which discouraged many teachers from participating. Even some fairly recently opened teachers' centres are housed in old nineteenth-century three-tier school buildings, which although they are well decorated and furnished are nevertheless still recognisable as former children's classrooms.

The building for the centre having been agreed upon and partially prepared, provision was made in the estimates for 1968/69 for the appointment of a half-time warden – he was to teach in a local school the other half of the time – and for that all-important British institution, a tea-lady; though no provision was made in the first year for any clerical assistance to the warden! So on the 1st May 1968 the Enfield Teachers' Centre officially came into being and a somewhat bemused mathematics teacher, now a warden, found himself with the job of making it spring to life!

Starting points

The most obvious starting point was to visit other centres which were already in being and ascertain more fully what their function was; how the warden saw his role; how they were equipped; what they did for the local teachers and how they saw their future. The most profitable of the visits I then made was to the Newham Centre and its leader of curriculum development – as the warden was called – Ernest Millington. This centre had already been active since 1964, having started its life as a Nuffield Mathematics Centre catering purely for primary mathematics; but by 1968 it had become a multi-purpose centre with considerable successes to its name. The most important factor that emerged for me from a day at Newham was that for a centre to succeed in attracting local teachers and involve them in the work of the centre, it must provide a service for teachers which met their real needs. This could manifest itself in a number of ways – through materials available free of charge for making visual aids for use in the classroom; through machinery – reprographic in the main – which individual schools could not justify purchasing but which teachers needed to help them with their work; through exhibitions at the centre of books, equipment, etc.; through a newsletter going out to teachers with information of immediate relevance to them; and even through such a mundane service as the up-to-date and clear displaying of notices and circulars of courses, jobs and other useful information. Having shown through this service that it had something of immediate value to offer to teachers while continuing in this supportive role to teachers, a centre could then also begin on the other important facets of its job – namely curriculum development and in-service education.

Centres have developed a broader and deeper philosophy than this earlier, somewhat superficial view of their need to hold out a carrot to teachers to attract them, but in the early days of the Enfield Centre the advice I had received at Newham proved to be most useful and it is still relevant in today's thriving centre.

The first task, therefore, was to show local teachers that the centre had something to offer them of value, to make the centre an attractive one and begin little by little to plan an overall programme. To discover what topics were in greatest demand for in-service education, which days teachers thought most convenient for attendance at after-school centre activities and what time of the evening suited them best, a questionnaire was sent to every teacher serving in the borough. The response by normal standards of replies to questionnaires was quite encouraging – some 20%-plus replies were received. The percentage response from primary teachers was high while that from secondary school teachers was very low, an omen for the future pattern of participation in centre activities.

From replies received to the questionnaire a league table of subjects requested was drawn up. At the top of the list from primary schools in the first year, and in every subsequent year when a similar questionnaire has been sent to teachers, have been art and craft, mathematics, science and reading. The presence of these four topics near the top of the league continues despite the fact that the centre has provided some excellent courses each year in each subject. The appetite of teachers for art and craft especially seems to be insatiable. Replies from the small percentage of secondary teachers who responded were spread over such a wide range of the curriculum that no significant topics emerged.

Concerning the most suitable days and times, the results were quite clear – any day from Monday to Thursday inclusive was equally suitable and, except for married women, the 4.30–6.30 p.m. period was preferred. Married women looked to evening sessions, after 7.30 p.m. when husbands could baby-sit for them. (The demand for late-evening courses by married women has been one which has only been met on a very few occasions in the life of the centre. Married women being a minority group in the borough, it is difficult to cater for them without inconveniencing the large majority who will only attend early meetings and courses. A surprising feature of the survey was the percentage of replies which indicated a willingness to attend holiday courses (30%), Saturday courses (23%) and courses during the half-term holiday (17%).

The resulting programme for the first and second terms of the centre's existence consisted mainly of exhibitions, discussions on the Plowden Report, Nuffield Mathematics for primary teachers, a reading course; and the best-attended meeting in the history of the centre, a demonstration of primary art and craft, to which 200 teachers came. Compared with the type of programme now offered each term it would almost appear that the centre was not used at that time. In the Summer Term 1968 there were 23 sessions compared with 136 in the same term in 1971 and the Autumn Term 1968 programme listed 62 sessions compared with more than 222 in the autumn of 1971.[2] These figures also give some idea of the explosion of activities once the centre was fully operating.

Management

The responsibility for advising the Chief Education Officer on the best utilisation of the centre was given to a Centre Advisory Committee. This consisted of:

The CEO (Chairman)
Education Officer – Secondary
Education Officer – Primary
5 teacher representatives – nominated by the Teachers' Committee and all members of that Committee
The Vice Principal of the Local College of Education (co-opted)
The Warden (Secretary to the Committee)
The Advisers (non-voting members)

Its present constitution remains the same with the exception of the co-option of the Assistant Education Officer for Further Education, as a non-voting member. This membership ensures that teachers have a majority voice in the policy-making body of the centre, a fact with which none can quarrel.

The selection of teachers to serve on a committee drawing up the policy for a teachers' centre in ideal circumstances would combine two different 'types' of teacher. On the one hand, members of a Teachers' Committee are usually the teachers most experienced in conducting discussion and meetings on behalf of their colleagues. This is one important quality required of a centre policy committee. On the other hand those teachers who are frequent users of the centre and its services can best evaluate the usefulness of the centre programme. Such teachers are also essential to a balanced committee. Since it is not always easy to find individuals who combine both qualities the ideal committee should endeavour to include a balance of the two 'types'.

The Advisory Committee meets once a term. In the early days of the centre all matters were referred to this committee but it soon became obvious that this was an impossible task and sub-committees were set up. The main sub-committee is that which deals with the programme. After a number of co-options, it consists of an infant, junior and secondary head teacher, the vice principal of the local college of education, a secondary teacher, two advisers and the warden (other advisers are welcome and attend from time to time). By virtue of the co-option, to which there is no limit, this committee does consist of teachers who use the centre regularly. It meets two or three times per term and is basically responsible for the successful programmes which the centre has operated for the last three or more years. In addition there is a social sub-committee – this runs the social programmes which take place two or three times per term; a library sub-committee – dealing with the purchasing policy for the centre library and spending three or four afternoons per term classifying and cataloguing the newly purchased books; and an editorial sub-committee which, with the warden as editor, brings out the termly newsletter. These three sub-committees consist of teachers actively involved in the work of the centre who have volunteered for the job.

The policy of the Advisory Committee and of the local authority with regard to the staffing and equipment of the centre has been one of a gradual build-up as a case could be made for increases on the basis of centre usage by teachers and general teacher demand. In my view this is as it should be. The alternative policy of beginning with a glorious edifice, fully equipped and with a large staff looking for ways to justify their existence, is not one to be recommneded. Beside its more obvious absurdities, such a policy would be counter-productive in the eyes of teachers who are fighting each day to obtain sufficient equipment and finance to enable them to do a better job in the classroom. The former policy does, however, have its drawbacks since local government is built around a yearly cycle of estimates and budgets. Thus any increase in allocation – staff or equipment – must always await the next financial year. With the rapid expansion of teachers' centre activities, this can have a braking effect which would be better avoided.

In terms of staff the build-up in Enfield has been continuous, starting with a half-time warden only, paid as a head of department Grade C (an allowance of £472 per year). After two years the post became full-time and was up-graded – in terms of salary – after three years to Scale 5 (£2,499–£3,277), equivalent to a Grade E head of department on the former scale. A similar build-up took place with ancillary staff so that in the fourth year the centre had reached the position of having a full-time clerical assistant to the warden.

The financial policy of the centre has allowed for an annual increase in the equipment housed at the centre. Each year, the warden, through the Advisory Committee, submits estimates for purchases of capital equipment required in the following year and for the revenue expenditure anticipated. On the basis of these estimates and the moneys made available by the local council for education in the borough as a whole an allocation is made to the centre. This has been, on average, in the region of £2,500–£3,000. Excluded are all salaries, lecturers' fees, and maintenance of the building, which come from central budgets and have always been adequate to meet the expanding needs of the centre.

The one commodity which is now in short supply after nearly five years of continuing expansion leading to ever more teachers using the centre and ever more meetings, courses and lectures, is accommodation. On many days during the term the number of rooms available is insufficient to meet demand and already rooms have been annexed in the very school building to which the centre was itself an annexe before 1968. An urgent priority in the near future will be the expansion of the actual premises of the centre, a problem which is already under consideration by a 'development' sub-committee. We are hopeful that in this matter local government administration will keep pace with consumer demand and that the development of centre work will not be retarded by the lack of sufficient accommodation. Credit must be given to the support received for the work of the centre from the local Education Committee, through its chairman. At all stages of our development, there has been a readiness on the part of the chairman and committee to give all the financial and staffing help within their power to ensure the continuing success of the enterprise.

The multi-purpose centre

Nationally, two broad types of centre exist: the single-subject centre, many of these dating back to the Nuffield Project as described by Professor Matthews; and the multi-purpose centre, originating from the Schools Council's suggestions in Working Paper No. 10. The Enfield Centre is multi-purpose. In my view it is only in a multi-purpose centre that many of the underlying philosophical tenets of teachers' centres can fully be realised. This is not to deny the advantages of the co-existence in any one area of multi-purpose and single-subject centres, each with their own part to play.

One of the basic premises of the teachers' centre philosophy, so far as such a philosophy can yet be defined, is the breaking down of barriers, a theory I have already advanced elsewhere.[3] The barriers which have all too long persisted in education in this country are between primary and secondary teachers; between individual subjects of the curriculum, especially in the secondary school; between teachers and head teachers; between the classroom practitioner and the college of education lecturer; and between the practising teacher and the administrators (inspectors, advisers and officers). In the multi-purpose teachers' centre there is no room for such divisions, no room for a hierarchical system. All meet together as equals with their own special contribution to make according to individual expertise.

The Enfield Centre's policy is to encourage the cross-fertilisation of ideas between all who make a contribution to the education of the pupils in our schools. This is achieved in many ways, the simplest being the idea of the centre as a common meeting ground where everyone can meet informally over a 'cuppa' or in the interval in a film show, etc. More formally, the programme is structured to encourage cross-fertilisation and activities are carefully planned, wherever possible, to cater for all categories of teachers – primary and secondary, head teachers and assistant teachers. The local college of education, both students and lecturers, are welcome to take part and the centre tries to co-operate with the college in its work. An excellent relationship also exists with the borough's advisers and officers, who play an active part in many aspects of the centre's activities. They in no way dictate to the warden or committees the lines of centre development, as happens in some authorities elsewhere usually to the disadvantage of the centre. I find that their advice and help are always available when called for and they participate in activities as equals with a special contribution to make.

Much has been said of late regarding 'change for change's sake' and teachers' centres have been accused of contributing to such a philosophy. It is certainly true that centres consider it as one of their primary functions to encourage teachers to examine and re-examine every facet of their work. However, such an examination in depth need not lead to the rejection of existing practices which have been effective for learning in the classroom. It could equally lead to a re-adoption of traditional methods which on critical examination have been found relevant to present needs. It could lead, and often does, to the working out, by teachers themselves, of new techniques. What is fundamental to the philosophy is not the act of change but the process of evaluation. It is this which is embraced in the term 'curriculum development'. It is here that the teachers' centre movement has revolutionised the mode of in-service education of teachers in the past few years. It manifests itself in the participatory forms of activity which are the bread and butter of teachers' centre activities and programmes.

The programme

With the basic tenets outlined above as its basis the activities of the Enfield Centre divide broadly into the following categories:

Lectures – the term is used to describe what is normally a non-participatory activity, the audience being restricted in the main to a few questions at the end. For this reason it tends to be used less and less in Enfield's programme. However, on occasions a lecture can serve as a useful introduction to follow-up activity by a working party examining the topic at further sessions, in depth.

Workshop courses – these are increasingly becoming the mainstay of centre activities. While new material is introduced by the tutor of such a course for consideration, every opportunity is given for discussion of practical work by the teachers participating and most importantly the chance is afforded for teachers to experiment in the classroom with the materials before returning to a subsequent session to discuss pupil reaction and to amend and modify the ideas in the light of this.

Working parties – to this type of activity there need be no 'in-put' in terms of a tutor or lecturer. It refers to a group of teachers meeting together to discuss a particular topic in the curriculum or a development in education. As a result they may produce materials for classroom use which will become available to other colleagues in the area; they may publish a report of their findings with recommendations for action; or they may call for some further activity embracing other teachers in the region. The success of working parties is entirely dependent on the group throwing up its own leadership in terms of a chairman and secretary. Where these teachers are willing to call regular meetings, plan, progress and ensure that the topics discussed are relevant the working party will thrive for the period required to carry out its work. Where the group is dependent on constant stimulation from the warden the success of the enterprise must always be in doubt.

Some examples may serve to illustrate the point: A working party on 'Decimal Currency and Metric Units of Measurement' produced useful information for teachers on equipment, and textbooks, organised exhibitions and courses, and was less instrumental in arranging a one-day closure of all primary schools when teachers attended a conference organised by the working party. This took place prior to the changes in British units which affected the entire content of mathematics teaching in the primary school.

'Leavers' Conferences'

This group worked continuously over four years planning conferences for the fourth-form pupils of local secondary schools on such topics as work, freedom, love and conflict. They experimented with new techniques for involving the pupils through discussion, drama, craft and other techniques. The emphasis was on a non-school atmosphere – activities were held in a youth club, with continual reappraisal and changes in the light of experience. The membership of the working party combined teachers, youth workers, college of education lecturers, and, most important, student teachers. These students came to play a dominant role in the conferences as the working party developed their mode of operation.

'Raising of the School Leaving Age'

This working party, which was formed as the outcome of a lecture, worked over a two-year period to produce an authoritative document with practical suggestions for teachers on the short-term and long-term solution of problems raised by the impending statutory raising of the school-leaving age to sixteen.

'The Role of the Class Teacher in the Practical Training of Student Teachers.' Two groups (comprised of teachers, advisers, officers and college lecturers) meeting to consider this question produced a report which considerably changed the concept of the work student teachers carry out in the classroom; it led to a new approach to 'probationer' teachers for whom a supportive programme of courses, meetings and opportunities for discussing private and professional problems with advisers and officers was initiated.

Other topics considered by working parties have been 'Entrance to and Transition from the Infant School', 'The Middle Years of Schooling', 'Sex Education', 'Modern Language Teaching in Primary and Secondary Schools' and 'Organisation and Human Relationships in Today's Comprehensive Schools'.

Exhibitions are organised from time to time to put on display work of particular interest done by pupils in one school, or work resulting from a workshop course at the centre. In bringing work to the attention of a wide cross-section of teachers such exhibitions have helped in the process of cross-fertilisation of ideas. Exhibitions of furniture, books and equipment have also been mounted periodically.

Associations. The programme of the centre also includes meetings of teachers' associations which were born out of teachers' centre activities. These have included three thriving groups, the Association of Pastoral Teachers, the Enfield Association of Remedial Teachers and a Careers Teachers' Association. While these are run by their own committees of active teachers their meetings are open to all teachers in the borough and again they have influenced the pattern of in-service work. They feed back to the centre suggestions for follow-up courses, etc.

Social. The primary functions of the centre have already been made clear, but in so far as time and accommodation permit the active social programme of the centre serves as a further opportunity for informal meetings for all concerned in education. The programme includes a weekly 'Open Night' when the centre is at the teachers' disposal until 11 p.m. for table tennis, bridge, television, chess, etc., and periodic functions from feature film-shows to folk evenings. On these occasions everyone – probationer, retired teacher and office administrator; foreign language assistant and adviser – all mix freely as equals.

Apart from these main ingredients of the centre programme which are initiated by the Advisory Committee, as space permits the centre is also used by advisers and officers for meetings and courses planned by them; by professional associations; and by committees of all forms.

Resources

An argument is put forward in some places for a separate 'Resource Centre' for an area. I personally don't favour such a policy. On the face of it, the arguments for resources being an integral part of the main centre are unanswerable. The case for resources acting as a magnet to attract teachers who might otherwise not visit the centre was already mentioned earlier. Experience on many occasions in Enfield has shown that this can lead to a teacher becoming involved in other activities of the centre. More important, however, is the inseparability of courses and resources. Many courses require the use of equipment of all sorts and as we go further into the age of technology this trend will increase. On the other hand a building housing only machinery, however sophisticated, is cut off from its life blood – the discussion and examination of how the machines can best be utilised to the benefit of the educational and classroom situation. This has led to a concentration of resources at the Enfield Centre. An exhaustive list would have limited value, suffice it to give some broad categories into which these resources fall:

Library. This contains books on current educational developments both in general categories across the subjects of the curriculum, viz. team teaching, mixed ability grouping, etc. and in individual disciplines. In addition a wide range of professional journals is displayed together with the catalogues of publishers, manufacturers and other related information. To ensure the availability of any book on any occasion a teacher may visit the centre to examine it, the library is available for reference purposes only.

Materials. Any teacher in the borough may come to the centre and using the art and craft materials available may make visual aids, work cards etc. for use in his school. All materials used are available free of charge.

Reprographic machinery. The centre has purchased a wide

range of machines – electronic stencil cutters, photo copiers, duplicators, etc. – mostly too costly and too specialised to merit purchasing by one school – which may be used by teachers, charge being made pro rata for materials consumed.

Audio-visual aids. A variety of audio-visual aids is available to schools to borrow for use on special projects, school journeys, etc. This includes cameras (still and 8 mm movie), projectors, tape recorders and a complete video-tape and camera system. Where the use of machinery is concerned the warden is available to teachers to assist and instruct them in its operation and regular courses in greater detail are run for the centre by the staff of the local technical college. These services to schools have been much valued by local teachers and it would now be difficult to envisage a system where they were no longer available.

Communications

The problem of good communications is crucial to the success of the teachers' centre. In finding a perfect solution unattainable the teachers' centre is far from unique in a modern society where the lines of communication are severely overloaded. However, it is essential that the warden uses every device possible to ensure that the teacher in every classroom in the borough is aware of what the centre has to offer him both in terms of resources and in terms of its programme.

To cater for this need a network of 'agents' in each Enfield school has been set up. These operate under the title of 'Teachers' Centre Correspondent' and it is their function to bring the information sent out by the centre to the attention of those of their colleagues to whom it is directed. That is, where a course has general application all the staff should be informed and where, especially in a secondary school, it has specialist application the members of that department have their attention drawn to it by the correspondent. Conversely, the correspondent keeps the centre informed of teacher reaction to centre activities and his colleagues' suggestions for further activities. The extent to which the correspondent is enthusiastic and effective can be the measure of a particular school's involvement in the work of the centre.

In the early days of the centre courses were publicised individually as the details of speakers, dates and times became available. Teachers found this system too piecemeal since it prevented them from planning their participation. At their request a termly programme is now published and circulated to all schools, available on the first day of each term. In this publication – *What's On* – the entire programme for the term is laid out together with application forms for each activity. When extra courses, due to overbooking or the need to follow up an earlier meeting, are provided, supplements to *What's On* are sent out during the course of the term. A measure of the increase in size and scope of the centre's activities may be indicated by the fact that the first *What's On*, for the Autumn Term 1969, contained five activities, while the comparable issue for the Autumn Term 1972 contained twenty-two plus a supplement of purely Audio-Visual Aid Courses with a further nine items.

The major publication of the centre is the termly *Newsletter*. This publication had also grown from small beginnings as a four-page initial issue in June 1968 to 46 pages in July 1972. Today it is not only read by the teachers in Enfield, but it circulates to other centres and individuals in all branches of the educational world in this country and abroad. It has come several times to the attention of both the national press and been quoted by a variety of educational publications.

Today, *Newsletter* consists of four main types of article. Firstly, two regular columns enable those concerned with education in the borough to get to know each other and exchange views. Thus, there is a termly profile of one of the borough educationists and an article 'I Believe' in which selected local people involved in education are invited to contribute their beliefs. The second section contains articles on current developments in education locally and nationally, while the third section contains reports of courses and meetings which have taken place at the centre for the benefit of those who were unable to attend. Finally, a fourth section contains reviews, in a column where schools are invited to recommend books and equipment they have found valuable; and a column 'Did You Know?' in which information about cheap or free materials and the sources where they may be obtained are listed. Discussion and correspondence is also encouraged for publication.

Newsletter at present prints more than 1,000 copies which in the first place are circulated to the staff rooms of local schools, on average five copies per school. Individual teachers may also opt to receive a personal copy and more than 200 teachers take up this opportunity. Local colleges of education receive copies both for the staff and the students.

The number of spontaneous contributions received for the *Newsletter*, together with the willingness of all those invited to make contributions, are a measure of this success – so that the editorial committee have found the size of each issue growing to almost unmanageable proportions. Reports of the working parties earlier described are published as supplements to the *Newsletter*.

Taking stock

After only some four and a half years of its existence it would be foolish to attempt to draw any conclusions about the work of the Enfield Teachers' Centre. In common with other centres in the country, it is still in state of flux, as the demands made on it change. In fact, it would be true to say that by the very nature of a centre it should never become a formalised institution, but must continue to move with the times and cater for the constantly changing patterns in education and in-service education. However, one fact is underlined quite clearly from the ever-increasing use of teachers' centre facilities and that is the crying need which must have existed in the past, prior to the introduction of centres, for a framework whereby teachers could participate in curriculum development and in-service education.

It must not be assumed from what I have written, however, that all teachers are equally involved in the centre or equally keen to attend courses and meetings. In the main the greatest response has come from primary teachers and the breakthrough to secondary teachers has been and still is an on-going struggle. There are many objective reasons for this – in a primary school all staff teach all subjects and are therefore in theory customers for a course on, say, mathematics, while in the secondary school only a small number of mathematics specialists exist and so the potential audience is smaller. Nevertheless, it is far more difficult to convince secondary teachers of their need for in-service education at centre level – and above all of their need to participate in curriculum evaluation and development. The situation has slowly improved over the past four years and there is a small but marked increase of interest among secondary teachers. It must also be made clear that not all primary teachers are equally involved. Clearly, there will always be a 'hard-core' of teachers both primary and secondary who will resist the helping hand the centre holds out to them. The vast majority of centre activities are held in out-of-school time. No element of compulsion can be introduced even if this were desirable. Though it must be said that there is demand by local head teachers for more activities in school time so that they can insist on a member of staff attending. Where this has happened in the past some notable conversions have been made with those involved suddenly becoming aware of what the centre has to offer them.

It hardly needs stressing that the role of the warden has altered considerably as a centre has developed. At the present time, what I most regret is the extent to which I have become an administrator who is no longer involved at any time in teaching in the classroom. This has two drawbacks, the personal one of losing touch with the reason the teachers' centre exists – the children themselves – and secondly the way it affects the image the warden presents to teachers, which ideally should always be that of another teacher. In the main it has been pressure of work rather than a clear policy that has created this situation, and given additional professional staff in the future, I hope that once again I can spend part of each week in the classroom.

There has been an increasing flow of educationists of all sorts interested in the development of teachers' centres in this country who have visited the Enfield Centre and other centres in the region from countries overseas. It would seem from their reactions that one might look in the near future to the centre movement spreading to a number of other countries. It is to be hoped that in adapting the ideas as they have developed here to their own needs a further advancement of the whole philosophy of centres will occur which in turn will feed back to this country, and thus in its turn promote further thought and development. Certainly, the experience of wardens working in centres in Britain has been that the cross-fertilisation of ideas between centres in a region and between regions has acted to the benefit of all. This has led to the development of regular contacts between wardens and the gradual emergence of a more formal structure on a regional and national basis embracing wardens.

Whether the authors of the Schools Council's Working Paper No. 10 could have envisaged the mushroom development of teachers' centres which their document initiated cannot be ascertained with any degree of certainty. In retrospect it can, however, be seen that the continually growing teachers' centre movement has in a period of little more than five years led to the new professionals – the centre wardens and leaders – becoming established as one of the strongest influences on the whole pattern of in-service education and curriculum development. Whatever the eventual fate of the suggestions for the 'third cycle' of teacher education, as the James Committee called the in-service education of teachers, wardens and teachers themselves will wish to see a continuation of the spirit of local support for teachers which has come to be the corner-stone of the teachers' centre philosophy. They will wish to ensure that teacher demand decides the pattern of the local in-service education programme and not a committee remote from the classroom dictating the programme from an ivory palace. The new professionals themselves must ensure that they remain as they were in the beginning – teachers, knowing and interpret-

Young teachers at a residential teachers' centre (Stoke d'Abernon)

Left to right: Mrs Julia Matthews, Professor Geoffrey Matthews, who led a course on nursery mathematics, Robert Thornbury and three nursery teachers joining in a nursery maths reunion

The result of a clay workshop, which was exhibited and to which teachers in the district were invited

Rachel McMillan College of Education annexe and teachers' centre, first building inset at right of picture—the city setting of a general purpose centre

ing the needs of teachers and giving practical support to their own colleagues.

REFERENCES

1. Working Paper No. 10: Curriculum Development – Teachers' Groups and Centres, published by H.M.S.O., 1967.

2.

No. of Sessions					
TERM	1968	1969	1970	1971	1972
SPRING	—	84	108	168	224
SUMMER	23	79	105	136	190
AUTUMN	62	110	140	225	222

3. Ideas, No. 23, October 1972, published by the Goldsmiths' Curriculum Laboratory, London.

6 *Regional Curriculum Development through local Teachers' Centres – some reflections*

BILL GREENWOOD

The Burnley Centre and the North West Project

I suppose that there are as many different types of teachers' centre as there are teachers' centres, and rightly so; a centre *should* reflect the needs of the area which it serves and also, to some degree, the personality of the person appointed centre leader. Having said that, however, I want to argue that being members of a Regional Project produced a degree of consistency of operation (some people would say conformity) within the cluster of centres established to facilitate the development of the ideas inherent within that Project, and that, in fact, being members of the North West Regional Curriculum Development Project stamped the centres, and therefore the centre leaders, as being something different.[1] The Burnley Centre was one of the 15 which were deliberately established to facilitate the Project and though my remarks specifically relate to my experience at Burnley they would be echoed, I am sure, by those of my colleagues who have been associated for a long time with the Project.

The exact details of the origin of the project remain somewhat of a mystery to me, though I suspect the Regional concept with Schools Council involvement came from the joint thinking of Derek Morrell and Professor Stephen Wiseman, while the detailed thinking related to curriculum development came from Dr W. G. A. Rudd, largely as a result of the experience gained in an earlier CSE experiment.[2] My personal knowledge of the existence of a Regional Curriculum Development Project, for the preparation of materials for ROSLA, came about as a result of reading a document *Forward from Newsom – A Call to Action,*[3] published in the Autumn of 1966: this document was prepared at Manchester University and distributed to each school within the Manchester Area Training Organisation and indeed circulated in schools in areas outside the Manchester ATO. The document had the backing of 13 LEA's,[4] and was designed to indicate a possible way in which such a Project could proceed. Closely following it came an advertisement for the post of a Curriculum Development Officer, whose task it would be to lead and service a teachers' centre. This centre was to be so situated as to cater for the teachers at secondary level in Burnley County Borough, together with teachers from Division 6 of Lancashire (the Nelson—Colne area) and from a single school in Division 5 (Padiham—Gawthorpe). This particular teachers' centre was to complement the fourteen others which were to function on a cooperative basis within the framework of the Regional Project. Upon applying for the post I was short-listed, interviewed and appointed, my appointment to take effect from 1st January 1967.

My thought at this time stand out clearly; I was eager to get to grips with the production of materials which *I* had mapped out in *my* mind; never mind phrases like objectives and evaluation. All I wanted was a pen, paper and a few sympathetic colleagues and the task would soon be completed. How wrong I was! My intuitive feelings in 1967 about the types of courses to be constructed have been borne out: but as a result of being involved in the Project they have been broadened, deepened and sharpened, as well as being translated into actual teaching programmes. I feel that I have moved forward in my thinking from those early days.

'Blacked' by the union

With the beginning of the Christmas holidays 1966, here was I, then, a young teacher, seconded[5] from the school where I had started teaching six and a half years earlier, to a job about which I knew very little. Needless to say, I was a little nervous and apprehensive. It was during this holiday that I received my first bombshell: the teachers' professional associations within the Project area were expressing serious fear about the lack of involvement of teachers in the committee structure which it was intended would guide the Project. The document *Forward from Newsom* had suggested that an advisory committee should be established and this committee would act as a second tier to a planning committee. The planning committee would consist of one representative from each constituent LEA, one HMI representative, one Schools Council representative, and Professor Wiseman from Manchester University. The planned advisory committee would have 4 teacher representatives among a total of 28 members. Is it any wonder that the teachers' professional associations had fears or that queries related to 'ivory tower domination of any new curriculum' to be developed were raised?

As a newly appointed centre leader, not yet in harness, it was a traumatic experience for me to find that the local secretary of one of these professional associations, under direction from his County Association, had sent out a circular to all schools, indicating that the North West Project and the teachers' centre were to be 'blacked' (this document has never been officially rescinded, to my knowledge). The union members were to take no part in the activities of the centre at all. As a result of this the opening of the centre was delayed and I returned back to school in January 1967 – not an auspicious start at all. What had I let myself in for?

Hurried behind-the-scenes negotiations, a confrontation and

some astute diplomacy (the knowledge of which I have only at second-hand) led to the Project being salvaged and put onto a footing which produced within the Project a kind of professionalism which ought to be applauded. There evolved a new concept of the Planning and Advisory Committee, invested in a body which became known as the Regional Steering Committee; this committee was to encompass a wide range of educational expertise but having at all times a built-in *majority* of practising teachers. The committee was to consist of 49 representatives, 27 of whom were to be teachers nominated directly by the professional associations. With this newly emergent concept of committee agreed by all parties, the Project got under way and I started work in the centre during February 1967, some six weeks behind schedule.

I have taken time over this introduction simply to show that what I believe to be good for the development of a new professionalism in education did not get off to a very satisfactory start. Once under way, it was clear that a great deal of good-will existed between all parties; but would that good-will have existed if it had been some task less urgent than ROSLA which had been under consideration? I like to think that it would.

What was in existence was a project with a £30,000 grant from the Schools Council (acting as a pump primer) with the thirteen local authorities willing to back up further development, not only with good-will, but with the hard cash which has proved to be many more times greater than the £30,000 the Council provided.

This willingness has all along proved a major factor about which the LEA's concerned ought to feel proud (without wishing to be condescending at all). In simple terms they were willing to 'put their money where their mouth was', an attitude to which the practising teachers respond warmly. This, I believe, if curriculum development is to become meaningful, is a vital factor in the development of good-will between administration and practitioners; good intentions are one thing, but such intentions require support.

After the initial troubles there came into existence a working partnership of many elements of the educational scene, producing a climate within the North-West favourable to the ideas outlined in the Schools Council Working Paper 10.[6] In retrospect, I believe the North West Project to be one of the few examples of the realisation of the ideas contained in that document.

Islands of neutrality

This then was the background into which I was thrust during the early months of '67. Certainly within the locality there was some ill feeling towards the Project. One head, in particular, felt it as an outside threat to what was happening in his school rather than seeing it as a co-operative venture to which the staff could contribute, and from which they could learn. From February until July (the area has the 'wakes' holiday peculiar to the North), my time was occupied in establishing myself within the schools in the area and generally setting up the centre.[7] The regional pattern of activities demanded that approximately 40% of my time be allocated specifically to work on Project ideas. I had few guilt feelings of not doing anything locally, that is in terms of the establishment of local groups, for I was selling the idea of the Regional Project to schools when I was in my home territory, ideas which were fed, strengthened and developed as a result of attendance at Regional study group meetings with my colleagues. Teacher attendance at the centre (counting heads) and the products of local groups were not my immediate concern during those early formative months. Looking back and comparing my situation with that of other newly appointed centre leaders outside of a Regional Project, I have been thankful. Coming to grips with the Regional Project and informing the schools as to what the Project was about took up my time. I did not hastily convene lots of study groups, in order to justify my existence, only to find that they fizzled out through lack of any real fuel. This pattern was not fortuitous, but was part of the concept which the Project Director was trying to turn into reality. If centres are to be effective within the field of curriculum development (if we are to bring about change rather than continuity) then the leaders, upon whom much depends, ought to be given the skills and knowledge which can lead to them being effective. Being a 'good teacher' is insufficient; it is important but it has to be supplemented by other skills and knowledge, related to an understanding of how groups function, a knowledge of current educational thinking and practice, together with some understanding as to what curriculum development might be all about. The planning of the Project ensured that the fifteen centre leaders, who were to act as agents on behalf of the Project, obtained a working knowledge at more than a superficial level, of the points just outlined. One question which remains is, where are those outside of a Regional Project to gain their skills and knowledge. Is there not some need for the in-service education of centre leaders?

I have mentioned that a certain amount of ill-will existed toward the centre but it was quite evident that the work of the professional associations in delaying the start of the centre had caused anger to emerge within a body of teachers in the area. It did not surprise me at all to find that during negotiations for the establishment of a committee to 'run' the centre, great feeling was brought to bear against any concept of a committee being based upon representation at 'teacher politics' level. What emerged was the idea that the committee should be comprised of representatives from each institution concerned with educating pupils over the age of eleven[8] together with two LEA representatives (one from Burnley Borough, one from Lancashire County Council), two primary school representatives and two head teacher representatives. Each institution was responsible for deciding its own representative and as a result the committee, when it met, was comprised of a good cross section of people one would expect to find involved in education *but* meeting in a 'neutral' situation. The power one could bring to bear was that related to curriculum matters and I would want to stress the need for such 'islands of neutrality' if the concept of the teachers' centre is to remain meaningful in terms of the development of a profession which is 'client-oriented'. Power structures have no part to play in the teachers' centre movement.

Early activity in the Project

During the first half year (February 1967 to July 1967) my work consisted of the following:

Local level – a. visiting schools and establishing relationships.

b. establishing a local steering committee.

c. attending a series of staff meetings to outline what the Regional Project was about–(this was undertaken within schools).

d. establishing the institution which would house the concept of the teachers' centre–buying furniture, fitting in shelving, putting up wall display boards, etc.

In general, I would say that I spent the majority of my time getting out to schools and being with people in the 'real' situation, where it all takes place, and where ultimately the success of a centre can be measured. This getting out and meeting teachers on their own doorsteps, I would argue, can be a crucial factor during the very early days when groups meet together and find themselves faced with all sorts of new fears, stresses and anxieties; the balance of good-will created by such earlier school visits can often carry a 'group' meeting in the local centre over the initial period when group breakdown is most likely to occur.

Regional level – a. meeting[9] with colleagues (head teachers, university and college lecturers, teachers, inspectors, advisers, HMI) in an effort to thrash out what general curriculum for average and below pupils should be concerned with.

b. learning how to lead groups by actually leading the discussions of (a) and watching my colleagues do the same.

c. gathering knowledge as to what education might be about and the new methods being used in schools.

The establishment of the Burnley Centre can only be properly understood when put into context, that context being the gathering momentum of the North West Project. The Project has

been criticised for being slow in getting off the ground; rightly so, but it often takes a long time to ensure that the foundations are sufficiently strong to determine that the rest of the building can continue without fear of collapse. Work on the foundations continued within the Project and within the centre, the two elements complementing one another as they had been designed to do.

From September to Christmas, 1967, a period of twelve weeks, teachers from all the fifteen centres gathered together for one day per week, in school time, to try and establish what have become known as 'specific objectives'. The result of the first phase (February–July 1967) had been a generalised statement relating to secondary education for average and below average pupils; the exercise in the second phase was to gather practising teachers together and for these people to try and identify just how they, in their ways, could contribute in specific terms to this general statement of education which had evolved. Twenty teachers representing nineteen out of a total of twenty-six schools and other institutions in the area covered by the Burnley Teachers' Centre attended this series of meetings. Of what value was this to the centre? It meant, I think, the following:

a. At least one person from somewhere near 75% of the educational institutions in the area was coming to terms with the whole question of Aims and Objectives. There was being trained for the centre a cadre of personnel who would disseminate within their own schools some of the ideas which were beginning to have an impact on the educational scene.
b. A significant point of contact was being made in all the institutions involved – the idea of a school correspondent at shop floor level was developing.
c. Such people were required, and indeed felt it their duty, to report back to their colleagues, at school level, and at inter-school level also, what it was they had been doing. It seems to me that this point is one which is not given enough emphasis in teachers' centres: if people are spend-

their time involved in regional or local work then I would argue that they have a responsibility to let their colleagues know upon what it is they have been engaged. Failure to develop this necessary communication of ideas can lead to the development of a kind of cult – an attitude of 'Curriculum development is only for the golden'. This is a criticism which I feel could be levelled at the way the Burnley Centre developed; there was in existence an 'in-crowd' – a large one admittedly and very knowledgeable about curriculum development in theory and practice, but nevertheless it existed and was probably influential in stopping some people from going to the centre. It may be that 'in-crowds' are inevitable, I don't know; if they are inevitable then it is good that the centre leader is replaced at regular intervals and makes way for the establishment of another and different 'in-crowd', for only in this way will the understanding, at depth, of what teachers' centres ought to be about, be extended to a wider proportion of the teaching population.

d. A partial understanding of the concepts of pluralism and professionalism as defined by G. Caston.[10] Teachers were working with people from other educational institutions on a one to one basis, debating and developing ideas which were the prerogative of no single person. It was the development of the idea that as people we all have expertise to offer and that it is essential, if education is to develop, for all concerned to enter into a partnership for the benefit of the 'clients'.

e. The idea of curriculum development being a necessary feature of the teacher's life both in and out of school time was given much credence. Such teachers as attended the meetings were released from school for one whole day per week: they were timetabled out. The local authorities might not have found replacements for the people involved but they did give their blessing for teacher release on the basis outlined. One could be unduly critical I think by saying that the authorities ought to have provided substitutes, but just as teachers are constrained, so too are LEA's. This particular point has in fact been answered, for some Local Authorities have provided extra staff for school in order to encourage release for work in the local centre.

f. A realisation by those involved that sitting around the table talking is one thing but translating the talk into some kind of product for use by one's colleagues is a totally different matter. This group had to produce a report and not only did the reports have to be produced but deadlines had to be set and kept if the plans for the third and fourth stages of the Project were to be met.

'Think big – act small'

The points I have just made relate to the benefits which the centre (and thereby the area) gained as a result of the second-phase activities of the Project from the involvement of teachers. What did I gain – as a person leading a teachers' centre?

a. I realised that people coming together in group situations meet for a whole host of reasons – some because it is time out of school, others because they are genuinely interested in what it is you have on offer, others because they think it will get them promotion, while still others come because they are looking for answers to be given to them. Whatever the reasons for coming together the group has to be welded together, has to become work-oriented, and has to see itself as producing an end product. Such end products will vary from the production of actual teaching materials, or the submission of reports related to the problems of introducing a new idea, to the simple preview of our materials coming on to the commercial market. The point is, however, that the group should know that they have an end product to work towards as well as those outside the group being able to discuss what the product is.[11]

b. As a curriculum development leader I realised that I would have to play a key role within the groups operating within the centre if success was to be gained. A realisation that time was a crucial factor led me to adopt an attitude which has since been described in the following terms:

'Do your market research,
Think big,
Act small.'[12]

This has meant that the Burnley Centre has concentrated on curriculum development in depth over a small area rather than being shallow over a wide area. Is it best to attempt to do things well within a small number of activities or to dabble over a wide array? It has been said in relation to this point that 'You pays your money and you takes your pick'. Do you, or are there more fundamental arguments which ought to determine what we pick?

Groups of teachers began to meet during this period (September–December, 1967) within the local centre but when I say that only three groups met regularly to study the following: 'Outdoor Pursuits', 'Immigrants' and 'Careers Guidance', then my colleagues, so adept at producing statistics showing ever increasing numbers of teacher attendances at the centre, will look at me askance. I am frightened when I hear teachers requesting help and being told that they 'can come to the centre whenever they like'. I am still of the opinion that the teachers' centre is a concept, not an institution, and that we should be looking to see what is happening in schools as a measure of success rather than counting heads through doors of centres. The warden, centre leader, call him what you will, is no longer a teacher; at the same time, however, he ought not to be perceived by teachers as being someone from 'the office'. He should be a 'thing' in his own right with skills and expertise which he can offer to people in need of such; if some of these skills are those which I have outlined then it is essential that the skills be made continually available to those utilising the centre. In order to extend the activities of a centre it would seem that it would be essential for the centre leader to train other teachers in the knowledge and utilisation of, for example, skills in running a group – that is, in fact, what was happening during our second phase; teachers and centre leaders were being trained.

In the case of Burnley, it was almost the case that every school had on its staff someone being trained in the use of such knowledge, skills and expertise as could be used in the school situation as well as in the teachers' centre. This had been deliberately planned, not at local level, but at regional level. In retrospect, I think that I could have extended the influence of this group of people to a greater degree than I actually did, for I am now of the opinion that some of the capital being created at regional level was not used to the full in the local centre.

The third phase

The third phase of the regional operation took place during the period January to July 1972, and it was a phase which was deliberately aimed at involving teachers. The 20 people I have just mentioned spent the Easter term informing their colleagues within the local area just what it was that they had been about. Some of those people coming to these meetings were disappointed. Where were the courses? Have you spent all that time talking about objectives? School life isn't about objectives and fancy jargon phrases. These were some of the points made against what the Project was trying to achieve and a further body of people, to supplement the 'non-interested element' and the 'we are not being told by outsiders' element became somewhat antagonistic—not to the centre, nor myself, but to the concept of the Regional Project. It was, however, extremely encouraging to me as an individual having the backing of this Project. Those who became interested in the Project became active participants in the centre's work, those who objected to the Project saw the centre as a means of developing their own 'thing'. It was really a question of 'heads I win, tails you lose', for the Project's support was support for the centre just as was the antagonism which the Project evoked.

This support for the centre by the antagonists of the Project meant that I had to be adept at providing alternative approaches to curriculum development. The Project throughout has based its approach on a classical interpretation of curriculum development.

a. the statement of objectives,
b. the selection of content,
c. the organisation of learning experiences,
d. the evaluation of the effect of a), b) and c) and the readiness to commence the cycle again if need be.

Such an approach is not the only approach however, in that the starting point for curriculum development does not always have to be a statement of objectives – it can be any one of the four elements of the cycle and the one to choose is the one which interests the assembled group at that point in time. What the centre leader has to be acutely aware of is the necessity to lead the discussions on from the starting point, ensuring that all four elements of the cycle are referred to, time and time again, so putting them into a relationship of the one with the other three. Content and learning experiences are, generally, much more meaningful to teachers and these will tend to be the starting points at the local centre level – this was very much the case at Burnley anyway. What we have to ensure is that we don't stop at content but that we do lead teachers round and across the four points of a diamond.[13] Who is to do this? – In my view it is the centre leader and any colleagues who have the necessary skill to do this (skills and expertise which are intuitive to some individuals but which for the majority of us have to be practised and learned). This is what the Project was certainly doing for the centre leaders during the whole period of time it existed, developing the necessary skills and expertise, but particularly was it so during the first two years of its life. This meant that as a group of centre leaders we were able to establish *some* working groups and offer them *some* working knowledge and skills which would allow *some* degree of success to be achieved in terms of our criteria.

The whole of one day each week and sometimes supplementary time as well was spent (by the centre leader) on studying the theoretical side of curriculum development and group dynamics, but at the same time marrying the theory to the practice which was developing within the Project and within our own local centres. These meetings of the centre leaders, together with the Project Director and Deputy Director, provided an excellent opportunity for us, as individuals, to discuss our problems, and fears, and to analyse our mistakes while at the same time being able to call on immediate help and advice to overcome such problems as were arising.[14]

Writing the courses

The first part of this third phase had been concerned with communication; the second part took on a totally different emphasis. It was from Easter to midsummer 1968 that teachers were requested to submit their own ideas as to what kind of courses ought to be developed which would incorporate the stated objectives and would satisfy the demands early leaving pupils would make on schools. Out of over one hundred suggestions received it was determined by the Regional Steering Committee (with a majority of practising teachers) that seven[15] curriculum areas would be dealt with at regional level. Then began what, as I saw it, was to be a competition between some centre leaders, including myself, to recruit from the practising teachers in the area covered by the centre as many people as one could to any or all of the proposed panels whose job it would be to produce curriculum materials. I certainly felt the urge to head the 'league table' of teachers involved in the regional panels which meant doing a great deal of 'tramping' to meet individuals and schools in order to recruit. The right effect, that of involving teachers in the development of materials at regional level, was achieved, but for the wrong reason. Having a large number of people from the Burnley Centre involved in the regional work imposed limitations upon the centre's activities; a science group established in September 1968 fizzled out by December because three key people were also committed to the Regional Project. Something had to go; these people were teaching, many of them as senior and key members of staff with all the problems associated; working one day per week (theoretically) in the Regional Project and attempting to initiate a local development group as well. The pressures were just too great and so the local group, in this case, fell apart, never to be resurrected. On the other hand, what I would call a successful group emerged within the local centre simply because that which was envisaged at regional level was just not for the people at local level. Teacher involvement worked both ways, by design.

It was then, as I see it, not until September 1968, some eighteen months after the centre had opened, that the centre really began to get under way. From September onwards the teachers in the area began to get to grips with the questions of what to teach, why teach it and how to do it, both at regional and at local levels. People were seen to be leaving school, taking time off and travelling to the regional groups deliberately scattered throughout the county or travelling to the local centre. People began to talk and this is what any centre must achieve. Did people talk enough and was a sufficient communications network established to encourage the dissemination of the ideas? The answer must be, I think not. Pockets of people became isolated and this is not good, though it is probably inevitable. I would react and plan differently, I think, if I had my time to come again. I would be less worried at this stage in time of justifying my existence and would spend more time in establishing a network which encompassed all. (But still it is easy to reflect that hindsight does not take into account all the personal anxieties which one possesses at any given moment in time.)

The release of teachers

This seems a suitable point to look briefly at the way the administrators played a significant role in the establishment of the centre. We have a much clearer picture of how schools, universities, colleges and H.M. Inspectorate can co-operate in the curriculum development movement; it is much less obvious how the pure administrators, if there is such a body, can contribute. Certainly within the Burnley Centre they played an important and encouraging part and deserve some credit. The administration encouraged the release of teachers from schools to work in the local and regional activities; they did not provide extra help in terms of substitute teachers but schools were circulated indicating that the office supported the principle; the LEA representatives on the local steering committee positively supported ideas which would include the principle of teacher release. At local level it was envisaged that activities would not require teachers out of school for more than a half day at a time but that the emphasis should be on the 3 o'clock until 5 o'clock meeting. The normal weekly pattern of events became such that on three days the 3 o'clock meeting was promoted while on the fourth day the full afternoon meeting was the norm. At regional level half-day release with weekend meetings during each term was tried out during the first year of actual course production (September 1968–July 1969), but this pattern rapidly became extinct simply because of the pressures which teachers found they had when they took upon themselves the mantle of curriculum developers. The request, to the administrators, to extend the half-day meetings to whole day meetings was readily accepted: it was at this time that as a centre leader I heard from other of my colleagues that some LEA's were deliberately putting extra staff into schools in an effort to encourage the release of staff for involvement in curriculum development work at both local and regional levels – a policy I could do nothing but applaud and hope that it would be extended to the schools in the area covered by the Burnley Centre.

I would like to expand this point a little further, for what is not being recognised quickly enough at national level is that the introduction of curriculum development, aimed at achieving 'change', has tremendous implications. Teachers involved in curriculum development require support of all kinds, but the greatest resource we can offer them is *time*. The Burnley Centre was a beneficiary of this concept which was a major feature of the Project and this realisation of the 'time factor' was picked up by a far larger proportion of schools, in a more positive manner, than I have yet come across in areas outside the Project. The involvement of teachers in 'innovation for change', though not new, demands in the present climate a serious physical commitment on the part of individuals and schools and it is up to the various institutions involved in education to provide the necessary supporting agencies. Engaging teachers in curriculum development, certainly within the Regional Project, imposed serious physical and mental pressures. I can honestly report several people with whom I became associated actually suffered this strain and it is towards easing it that the local teachers' centre warden/leaders should direct their resources. It may be that the greatest service which we can provide to the teachers is in relation to 're-charging the spirit' of those who become involved; I sometimes wonder about the value of reprographic or library facilities when what is wanted is the person who can provide that kind of support required when the human spirit is flagging. In other words we should be aiming at the professional ethic outlined by Geoffrey Caston; the regional venture, based on this philosophy, though it had not been spelled out by 1966 as clearly as it has by 1972, turned it into practice. The regular weekly meetings of centre leaders within the Project were concerned at extending this argument while the whole of the administration of the Project was concerned at providing the necessary support for the concept of curriculum development to be turned into practical situations which caused teachers and schools to change. It is being publicly stated that the LEA's put £200,00 into the Project from 1967 to 1972 but I would suggest that in fact this figure is very much on the low side; the hidden costs have been tremendous and no one will ever be able to calculate the total cost of the Project.

It took a great deal of courage on the part of the administrators in the various LEA's to set up such a venture but the point I wish to stress is the need to make reasonable projections of the amount of 'support' which will be required before embarking upon either local, regional or national curriculum develop-

ment. Once a decision has been made there is then the need to back that decision up. I have a feeling it is better not to embark at all than to establish something which will be no more than a 'botch up' – we ought to return to

'Do your market research,
Think big,
Act small,'

simply because there are *limited* resources and we ought, for the sake of the clients, to do that upon which we embark, well.

The day the roof caved in!

Recently I read two very contrasting articles related to teachers' centres and curriculum development and I must say that I warmed towards *one* of them, which talked about innovation and curriculum development in an area where teachers' centres did not exist. It was by accident rather than by design that I gradually arrived at the notion of the teachers' centre, as an institution possibly being a barrier to innovation. To reiterate, the teachers' centre should be a concept, not an institution; and I wonder, will the teachers' centres as they become 'bigger, with more physical resources and staff' lose the idealism which the concept embodies? Could it be that institutionalising the concept will kill the concept? As I say, I have arrived at this quite fortuitously, simply because the Burnley Teachers' Centre consisted of one small room in a primary school. What sort of meetings can you hold in a room some forty-five feet long and twenty-five feet wide, where one corner is taken up as an office (six feet square), and a second taken up with the sink, geyser and duplicator? This left a space into which one could get an open square of tables, accommodating some twelve people, while the walls were suitably covered with display board. Adequate car parking facilities existed (much more than was the case for some of my colleagues) but the physical situation meant that we had to meet elsewhere – in schools (both in and out of school time). Curriculum development is about schools and teachers 'changing'; what is significant is not what goes on in the teachers' centre but what effect this has upon schools and the ways in which these function. What better place to hold meetings which attempt to initiate change than in the places which ought to be the recipients of the new ideas. I am not decrying all the arguments which one can put up for the existence of the teachers' centre, a comfortable place to meet, holding the necessary resources teachers need. What I am saying is that in the last resort, what counts is people, and I feel that the way the movement is going at the moment then we might forget about them. Resource banks and reprographic systems are only elements in the whole process and not the process itself – but I fear that they could become the be all and end all. It was a salutary experience for me when the roof of the centre caved in and for a full term it was not possible to do anything in the centre except use it as the base from which I worked. Does the pace of change in schools slow down when the teachers' centre is out of operation as an institution, when the wine and cheese parties, the dances, the buffets, the film study groups and so on cannot be held in the designated premises? Perhaps I am tending to polarise the situation, but I certainly feel that the 'mendicant friar', getting among the people where it is all happening, is more likely to cause change to occur than is the 'institutionalised bishop'.

The next phase of the North West Project commenced in the September of 1968 when all the teachers who had volunteered to work on the seven[15] designated 'curriculum areas' met for a working weekend at Padgate College of Education. Some 22 teachers from the Burnley Centre were to commence work on the task of constructing courses away from the local teachers' centre. The initial weekend was followed up with the different panels meeting in different teachers' centres; the domestic studies panel for example held their weekly meetings at Salford Teachers' Centre; the panel members had to travel to this centre which meant three teachers from the Burnley Centre were leaving the area behind and carrying out their tasks away from the local area. What was important, however, was what they brought back to the school and what the Burnley Centre could draw upon for the benefit of other local schools if the need arose (which it did frequently). The communication varied from the use of the centre as the focal point of dissemination, to the schools actually visiting the persons who were working in the development of the materials.

Later phases of dissemination and production

Dissemination of the Project and its products was built into the Project from its inception because of the planned teacher involvement. In the same way that centres claimed to be breaking down barriers between classrooms and schools, so the Project broke down the barriers between LEA's and between teachers' centres. Inter-centre co-operation, as well as inter-LEA co-operation, was an essential feature of the Project. Migration of teachers at a professional level has long been practised, so much so that at local level it has been possible to establish groups of teachers from a couple of centres working on a co-operative basis outside of the regional project. I smile when I read about the formation of a 'group' of wardens as though it were something new; the political emphasis of such a group may be new but the professional element has been part of the North West Project since its inception in 1967. The value to me of this inter-LEA co-operation at teacher and centre leader level is immeasurable but it could well be a pattern worth copying much more extensively than it has been.

The pattern of the Project from September 1968 was:

September 1968–July 1969. Development of materials – fourth year

September 1969–July 1970. Trial of materials – fourth year

September 1970–July 1971. Re-write fourth year materials. Development, fifth year

September 1971–July 1972. Trial of fifth year materials, fourth year materials published

September 1972–July 1973. Re-write fifth year materials for publishing.

I present this timetable in order to indicate the long and consistent drain upon the local centre of some of the most able teachers to work within the Regional Project. But so what? The important element is that such teachers have been involved in curriculum development and taken their expertise back into schools, just in the same way that colleagues have been involved in curriculum development at local level and taken their expertise back into schools. The complement of these two factors is that I found myself acting more and more in a consultancy role with individual schools within the area than I did working in the centre. I think that it is to this end that we should be aiming – the consultancy role. We can work on curriculum reform within the local teachers' centre setting, *but* if we are to change the schools then it is within the total setting of the school where we must work. It is not easy to reach the consultancy level – it takes time and an acceptance of the value of the centre leader by the schools and the teachers within the area the centre serves. Some people will never see or accept this as necessary and this is inevitable but it is towards this end that we should be aiming.

The second reason for spelling out the regional programme of activities is to indicate that panels of teachers had to come to terms with producing materials and ultimately publishing materials and this applies to activities at the local as well as regional level. It is, however, at regional level that we may have to give greater recognition to this question of publishing simply because it is a question of availability of resources. If teachers are going to meet together, on a regional basis, then their products, even though I would attach only minimal importance to these, as opposed to the process through which the individuals have been, ought to be made available. The products of the North West Project represent a way of organising materials together in a particular way (not necessarily new materials); the pattern indicates what materials a group of teachers decided could be used in a specific way to achieve certain outcomes.

Such materials ought to be presented to the pupils in the sophisticated manner to which the pupils are accustomed in this day and age; this means, of course, drawing upon all the expertise available from the publishing field. One must remember, however, that publishing companies are primarily commercial undertakings. What happens, when that which teachers and others involved in education have been working upon is rejected as being commercially unviable? How are the ideas and materials to be made available to the wider public, assuming that the work has a wider significance; who is to invest the necessary capital to ensure the production? It seems to me that if teachers are to be involved in curriculum development then one of the implications which those possessing the resources have to consider is how do we ensure that ideas and materials produced reach the schools other than by the commercial entrepreneur. Will the local authorities take it on themselves to provide the necessary resources or are we to have to place ourselves at the mercy of commerce? From experience I can say that it is difficult to reject publishers' demands to alter material because they consider it will not sell. If we are talking about a professional ethic based upon the clients then we must reject the commercial pressures and develop that which we consider best for them. The corollary of this is the establishment of a system of publishing entrepreneurs who are free from the profit motive;[16] are the LEA's the ones to take on this role? Could it not be that another form of co-operative venture between those involved in education is required: just as people have co-operated in the development of new courses could we not also extend this into the actual field of the production of classroom materials? This particular point is becoming increasingly evident when one looks at the National Projects which concern themselves with teacher involvement. The Burnley Centre, for example, was associated with the mathematics for the Majority Project and the teachers' meetings began to produce their own materials for use in the school situation. We spent a great deal of time drawing together the resources, in terms of reprographics, to produce a fairly sophisticated set of materials for use by the pupils *but* after the initial production was exhausted (the materials were expendable) who was then to continue the production? As a centre we ought to have been moving into new areas of development but the materials we had produced were insufficient in terms of quantity for a publisher to take over. It seems to me that these are serious considerations which the new local government units need to look at; but what of the effects upon the centre?

Co-operative professionalism

May I make one final point before attempting to draw together a few threads and that is the relationship between curriculum development and in-service education. I have been criticised before because of my attempts to draw distinctions between the two but I feel it is necessary. Let me say that the two are most definitely interrelated but they are distinct; in-service education is passive, concerned with input, whereas curriculum development is dynamic and is concerned with output. In-service education, often used as a starter, can lead to curriculum development, while curriculum development often necessitates some kind of in-service education. It is the curriculum development element, with its creative involvement of individuals, with which centres should primarily be concerned; it is the involvement in creating which will give the teachers the new horizons and strengths necessary if the teachers' centre movement is to be concerned with 'innovating for change' rather than 'innovating for continuity'.

Nothing in education is ever entirely new; teachers have always been reviewing the aims of their work, devising new courses and improving their classroom practice in the light of on-going experience. Such changes have usually been made by isolated individuals; but this practice suited a society whose expectations of its public education were suitably modest. As society has become rapidly more complex and the expectation of education more extensive, then fresh networks for allowing re-thinking and changes in practice have become necessary. It is in this situation that teachers' centres have developed and it is to this which we must aim at all times. Teachers' centre empires are irrelevant. What is important is how the centre helps the schools and individuals to come to terms with their re-thinking and the development of materials to match their re-thinking. It was as part of such a network that the Burnley Centre was established, a network where leadership and ideas emerged from different focal points.

This has been the great value of the Burnley Centre, being part of a whole; a whole based on innovation for change, the development of a client-centred professionalism and a whole which believed that if curriculum development is to become meaningful then no single body possesses the answers but that answers can be found by all strata of education co-operating together.

1. (or am I kidding myself that as a group of centre leaders we were given skills and expertise which made us something different from other colleagues establishing teachers' centres.)
2. See Schools Council Examination Bulletin, No. 20 – C.S.E. – A Group Study Approach to Research and Development.
3. Now out of print.
4. The thirteen LEA's in question were Bolton, Blackburn, Bury, Burnley, Blackpool, Lancashire, Warrington, Salford, Manchester, Rochdale, Stockport, Oldham, Westmorland.
5. The position was initially for two years with the possibility of extension if necessary; in fact at the time of writing I am into my seventh year of secondment.
6. See Schools Council Working Paper, No. 10 – Teachers' Centres.
7. I was fortunate enough in the respect that I was from the locality; even though I had taught in a school in division six of Lancashire I had a relationship with most of the schools in the area as a result of being actively engaged in out-of-school activities. My soccer and cricket contacts were to stand me in good stead: I hesitate to think what I would have made of the task had I been an outsider as it were.
8. In 1967 this consisted of a total of 6 selective schools, 3 special schools, 2 Colleges of Further Education, 14 Secondary Modern Schools and 1 College of Art.
9. Such meetings were held on two days per week for the period February–July 1967.
10. Journal of Curriculum Studies, Vol. 3, No. 1, May 1971.

11. Such end products will vary from the production of actual teaching materials, the submission of reports related to the problems of introducing a new idea to the simple preview of our materials coming on to the commercial market.
12. Lecture given by Brian Davies of London University.
13. See Taba, H., *Curriculum Development: Theory and Practice*, Harcourt Brace and World, New York.
14. It was during this period also that it began to dawn upon me that just as I was using the regional group for therapeutic purposes then so too could I expect teachers to come to the centre for exactly the same purpose. Any contemplation of work in the sense of production of materials or ideas has to take a back-seat until those within the group have got off their chests that which is bothering them. This brings me back to the concept of the teachers' centre being the 'neutral area' in which this sort of activity can take place. The centre leader should be able, out of necessity to what curriculum development is about, to take on that role which I best describe as 'the Mary Grant/Marjorie Proops role'.
15. These areas were as follows a) Technology, b) Social (including Health Education), c) Creative Arts, d) Moral Education, e) Domestic Studies and f) Team Teaching.
16. The ILEA Media Resources Centre is worthy of consideration in this context.

7 *Professional Support for the City Teacher*

R. G. GOUGH

Teaching down the Old Kent Road

Curriculum development is a luxury. This may seem like heresy in a book devoted to teachers' centres, but I will try to suggest that whilst it is not true, neither is the statement exactly untrue.

We all tend to get carried away by our enthusiasms, and visitors to teachers' centres, and people seeking information with a view to opening new ones, are often given the impression that having designated a building 'Teachers' Centre', people will flock to it in great numbers, form themselves into groups, and instantly commence to develop curricula. It is not as simple as that. Any slight movement towards change (and only genuine change is being considered – others have referred to 'innovation without change') has, in my experience, been the result of a long and arduous process during which the warden, at various times, takes on the mantle of public relations officer, teacher, philosopher, friend, bully . . . to say nothing of the *way* in which he plays these roles, which at times approaches the style of Machiavelli.

Apart from this, it seems to me that there are certain prerequisites necessary before any group of teachers can meaningfully engage in processes to bring about curriculum change. These prerequisites are probably in operation everywhere, but they perhaps have a particular force in the 'inner city' areas, and they are all to do with *teacher morale*. The teachers in Southwark (an area which includes inter alia Bermondsey, Camberwell and the Old Kent Road) are teaching children in circumstances where the effects of industrialisation and urbanisation have been concentrated and this is frequently reflected in the school buildings. The teachers here are as good as those found anywhere and – you must excuse my chauvinism – better than most. They are faced daily with children whose background is frequently, though perhaps inaccurately, described as 'deprived'. What is certain is that a large number of these children have not had, and do not have, the advantages of their peers in other areas. 'Unadvantaged' may be a more useful term than 'disadvantaged' in this respect. The teacher under such circumstances can perhaps be forgiven if he believes, for example, that eight-year-old Mary having had no breakfast is more important than her grasp of the Distributive Law, is perhaps more important than an exploration into different methods of teaching of reading.

Some of us who are involved in the provision of resources for 'in-service education' prefer that phrase to 'in-service training', since the latter has the connotation of programming the teacher with the latest 'message', or giving him his injection of Nuffield Physics, or whatever, directly into the vein. We mean something more dynamic, something more lasting, something more teacher-created, and we try to consider the needs of our teachers in terms of support. I believe it is our duty to provide a system of support before we can ask the teachers to give time and effort to coming to grips with the implications of what has been called 'The Changing Organisation of School Knowledge'. (This phrase too is preferable to 'Curriculum Change', since it gives a more embracing conception of what school knowledge is than is suggested by the everyday educa-

tionist concept of curriculum. Also the formal curriculum is only one aspect of school knowledge, albeit an important one.)

At the Rachel McMillan Teachers' Centre this aspect of our work is particularly manifested in a scheme for teachers in their first year of service. Our scheme involves allocating probationers in groups of about eight to 'tutors' (usually head teachers, but not invariably so) who are their guide, mentor and friend for this first year. (They are never allocated to the head teacher of their own school.) These groups meet for the first time at an 'Induction Day', held usually about three weeks after the autumn term has started. On this Induction Day, the probationers are released from school and attend at the teachers' centre, where they are introduced to various key figures in their support system; their tutors, local authority inspectors, teachers' centre staff, etc. They are also given information about the particular problems of teaching in this area, and take away with them a folder containing information specific both to Southwark and to the probationary year (e.g. details of what their salary should be, and what to do if something goes wrong; information about library and other resources; notices regarding professional associations and the like).

Finding somewhere to live

On the first occasion we carried out this exercise some four years ago, it was discovered that no less than ten of these teachers were sleeping on somebody's floor. They were from out of London, and accommodation was (and is) a problem. This event underlined for us the philosophy we were in the process of formulating. You really cannot expect a teacher to become engaged in a meaningful, effective way in the 'development of curriculum', or anything else, when he has nowhere to live, and is sleeping on a floor. Since that time an integral part of the teachers' centre service to teachers has been an informal accommodation bureau. We have sought from teachers information regarding flats (apartments) available. Typically, for example, three lady teachers sharing a large flat might lose one who gets a job elsewhere, and they are seeking a replacement. Thus the accommodation we advertise is 'teacher researched'. At the time of writing, we have a small excess of accommodation available, so, in a sense, that is a problem we have solved! There are, however, plenty more for us to work on.

This example of teachers' centre activity was an extreme, of course, but it illustrates that teachers in the inner city situation have particular needs, which have to be met before they can reasonably be expected to become involved in their own in-service education. Next, if in-service education is to be effective, then the teachers themselves must be deeply involved in the planning and organisation of its nature and content. There is a major problem to be overcome here, because teachers are not very good at articulating their needs. This is probably due in part to the pressures which are on the teacher, which give him little chance to stand back and indulge in self-examination. One of the jobs a teachers' centre must do is to try to provide such opportunity. Probationer teachers are even worse than average in indicating their needs, probably because of the particular nature of the pressures upon them. When a group of new primary teachers are gathered together after a few weeks' teaching and asked what is it that they need (expressed often as 'What courses do you want?'), they are in a state of confusion, since often they have not yet formed the kind of relationships with pupils and colleagues which are necessary in order to be effective in the school. At such a time they will verbalise a request, in terms of something they perceive as their evident failure, and so it is not untypical for requests for courses in 'Primary Mathematics' or 'The Teaching of Reading'. This has been interpreted by some observers as indicating a failure of the Colleges of Education – ('What have the Colleges been doing for the last three years . . . ?') Any such facile interpretation (or such readiness to find a convenient scapegoat) is not very helpful. These requests from young teachers are cries for help – but they rarely, in my view, reflect the latent needs of the teacher in the way they are expressed. What we have to do is to try to get below the surface of the stated requests to the underlying problems. In the case of probationers, these are often uncertainty, lack of confidence, and isolation. When they find that someone else in a school down the road, with a similar class, is having exactly the same difficulties, their problem is already put into a different perspective. If the probationers are meeting in a group with a skilled and sympathetic tutor, many of these mutual problems can be explored at an early stage.

Communications flow

To involve teachers in their own in-service education requires a massive exercise in *communication*. This has proved an area of major difficulty. How to get the appropriate information to the appropriate people at the appropriate time is, of course, a problem not confined to education. Nor is the amount of paper generated. This flows into schools day by day in vast quantities, as it does also throughout industry and commerce. We need to add to the flow to advertise our presence, and yet, paradoxically, we are aware that each increase in the amount of paper is likely to be counter-productive. What this means is that we must try to promote as much face-to-face contact as possible. A warden in an area in which there are about 150 schools and about 2,000 teachers could clearly spend *all* his time in schools, and still not make sufficient continuous contact with teachers. He needs, of course, to spend a lot of time in schools, but it is also evident that he must spend a lot of his time at the centre and elsewhere. One way we in Southwark have attempted to promote better communication is to have, in each school, a person designated as 'Teachers' Centre Representative'. All of our material – and in common with most other centres we produce a bulletin ('Centre News') indicating the nature and timing of in-service activites at the centre – is sent to schools via this teacher to whom it is addressed *by name*. Meetings are held regularly of those teachers' centre representatives, to which they are invited to bring along items from their staff rooms for discussion. We hope that by this means teachers are involved in the decisions regarding the content and process of their own in-service education.

Information from these meetings is supplemented by other sources in providing the material necessary in order to plan the programme of in-service activity organised by the teachers' centre. In common with the other multi-purpose centres in Inner London, we have our Advisory Committee. This has a formal constitution, determined after consultation by the Authority. The committee consists mainly of 'political' representatives, i.e. representing the various teachers' organisations and groups. In my case, the power of co-option has been used to ensure the presence on the committee of a) young teachers and b) teachers who actively use the centre. In the nature of things, representatives of teacher organisations tend to be very experienced (they are usually head teachers). Their experience is often of value, but what is often even more useful are their communication networks. There is no doubt that such people can wield influence in the area, and they can be very useful in the dissemination of ideas from the centre. It would not be unfair to say, however, that by and large such committees have not yet found a completely valid role. One would hope that, in time, when the rationale of teachers' centres becomes more evident, these committees will take an even more active part in helping determine the nature of the in-service activities for the area.

Probably the most important source of ideas and information from teachers regarding their in-service requirements is the detection system of the warden and his staff. The antennae here are crucial – and in visiting schools, sitting in on discussion groups and workshops at the centre and elsewhere, and in listening to teachers talk on all possible occasions, the warden begins to formulate teacher needs (and, incidentally, by these means the skilled warden can begin to discern the latent, often unexpressed, needs of teachers, as distinct from the manifest, apparent, needs. The latent needs are often concerned with important underlying sources of difficulty.). Another important source is the on-going activities. If these are not fulfilling a need, then our teachers will 'vote with their feet' – especially so since most of the activity we are discussing takes place after school hours in the teachers' own time. If you are not satisfying their requirements, they'll let you know – by staying away! These various ways of attempting to detect the needs and wants of teachers (supplemented, in the case of probationers, by the tutor-groups) demand quite an expenditure of time and effort. This expenditure is essential. Any attempt to short-circuit the process by the use of, for example, a postal questionnaire is not likely to be very fruitful. I suppose we all used questionnaires in the early days of teachers' centres – and no doubt they were useful at the time. A questionnaire today of reasonable length would probably only tap the surface of teacher-need (assuming adequate response!). Anyway, to replace the various processes just described would require a questionnaire of such length and complexity that no one would have the time to fill it in. We in Southwark do, in fact, use questionnaires – but they are *very* specific and very short. We might ask, for example, what specific courses primary teachers would like to have in, say, music. We might specify tuition in recorder, guitar, etc. . . . courses on Carl Orff materials, and ask for other alternative requirements. But these questionnaires do no more than complement all of our other channels of communication from teachers.

Teachers' centres in a college of education

It is obvious that lack of communication is a barrier to progress, and this is often reflected in a lack of knowledge of the possibilities open to teachers. These deficiencies may spring also from an attitude of mind. The teachers' centre in Southwark is based in a college of education. One of the barriers which had to be overcome here was the very substantial one existing in the minds of many teachers vis-à-vis colleges of education. There were those teachers who said to me that the Authority must have taken leave of its senses, otherwise they would never have based an institution like a teachers' centre in a college of education. My appointment was (and is) a joint one – half to the college of education as a lecturer in the education department; and half to the Authority as warden of the teachers' centre: I took my brief as attempting to meet teachers' needs, and I very quickly discovered that if you were providing something for teachers that they needed, wanted – it didn't matter too much where the activity was based. It would certainly be true that today – as far as what goes on in most teachers' minds is concerned – the fact that the particular building is also a college of education is not relevant, one way or the other. It is not a factor in the decision of whether to take part in a certain activity.

That the centre and the college of education share a building *is* important in many ways. The building is used as an annexe to Rachel McMillan College, and at this annexe a part-time teacher training course for mature students takes place. Since it is part-time (10 a.m.–3 p.m.), it means that all of the accommodation is available for teachers' centre use after 4 p.m. – when most of this activity takes place. Dual use means effective use of plant, which must benefit the tax payer (and as a tax payer, I welcome it). The centre was set up here in September 1968, and right from the beginning we have tried to build in flexibility of use and complementarity in equipment, so that both the college and the teachers' centre benefit (i.e. both students and teachers benefit). This is particularly evident in the media resources department which contains aural and visual aids materials belonging both to the college and to the teachers' centre. In 1971, the college and the teachers' centre collaborated in the appointment of a Media Resources Officer, who has a joint appointment – half to each institution. Under his guidance, the media resources department has developed and, with contributions from both college and teachers' centre, there is now a collection of resources which would be difficult to match in any other teachers' centre.

A further, related development is the arrangement now made with the college library, by which teachers in the area now have access to both the books and to the non-book resources collection being established. The centre makes contributions to the library from time to time, but these are catalogued with the existing materials. Apart from the books – and, obviously, there is a good collection of educational books – teachers thus have access to a superb range of magazines and journals (including back copies) which would not be possible otherwise.

It should be evident by now that I believe that there is considerable benefit obtained by basing this teachers' centre in Rachel McMillan College of Education. No one should go from this, however, to the notion that the only – or the best – place to base a centre is in a college. We have worked out a happy working relationship (though it hasn't been without its storms), but other centres in other areas do many things very effectively, and may well demonstrate strengths that we do not. What I have tried to indicate is the possible benefit from such collaboration. The disadvantages – apart from teachers' initial reluctance to have any truck with something labelled 'college of education' – lie mainly in the impossibility of the task of the warden. In such a situation, it is essential (I would argue) for the warden to have a designated (and significant) role in the college. Being thus clearly 'of' the college, as well as 'in' it, he is in a position to be aware of the points of friction, before the amount of heat produced is too great to be readily dissipated. He can anticipate the difficulties involved in working out the details of the programme in so far as they affect the college tutorial and administrative staff. He can do these things in a way that a person who worked on the premises only as a warden would find difficult.

'If you can't stand the heat, stay out of the kitchen'

The problem is that the demands of in-service education in such an area are continuous, are increasing, and are never satiated – and this will be more true in direct proportion to the success of the teachers' centre. Consequently, the warden if he is concerned to be deeply involved in the provision of in-service resources for teachers (and if he isn't, he shouldn't be a warden) could easily spend all of his time and more on the task. If half of his time is devoted to the provision of initial training, and he is also timetabled for lectures, seminars (together with his full share of those committees and boards, which seem an inescapable element of the twentieth-century life, not least so in education), then no amount of assistance in the form of deputy wardens or secretaries or whatever will do more than partly alleviate the pressures on him. And inevitably, if the deputy is energetic and capable (and mine scores highly on both counts) then a whole range of provision for teachers which was not possible even to contemplate before now becomes possible – and so the amount of work to be done becomes more than twice what it was before the deputy arrived. So the pressures on the warden become even greater and not less. If this sounds like a complaint, I must entreat you to believe that it is not so. I would be extremely worried if I was not overworked – if I had time on my hands. I would interpret this as failure. But whilst teachers continue to seek out help, whilst they continue to attend courses, workshops and discussion groups, whilst they continue to make such demands, I will take it as some small measure of success. Besides, as Harry S. Truman once said, 'If you can't stand the heat, stay out of the kitchen'.

It is useful sometimes to think of a teachers' centre in terms of *evolution*. When a centre is first set up the teachers in the area do not know what kind of animal it is, and are far from sure as to how to approach it. It is not unusual for teachers at this stage to perceive their needs almost entirely in terms of 'topping up'. They want to come along to the teachers' centre for their injection of Nuffield Mathematics or of Integrated Studies. Satisfying this apparent need for 'topping up' may well have more to do with teacher morale than with in-service training, but it is clearly an activity demanded at an early stage, and, if only because of teacher mobility, it is an activity which must clearly continue. These 'topping up' sessions may be viewed as the provision by the centre of someone with a message ('the fix'?), who injects it into the teachers, who go away apparently satiated. To continue the narcotic analogy, the benefits are found to be short-lived. The teacher might well come away with something he can do with his class the following day – but without reinforcement, without follow-up, he will soon begin to suffer 'withdrawal symptoms'. He might seek further 'topping up', but soon it becomes evident that this kind of dependency is not healthy in the long-term. Another stage in the evolutionary process, therefore, is the need to develop from the 'topping up' situation towards involvement by teachers in their own in-service education. This involvement must be established at all levels in the process – detection of needs; initiation and design of activities; carrying out of the activities; evaluation . . . This is far from easy. Apart from considerations of *time* – and in the urban situation teachers are under continual stress, and finding additional time for such activity is difficult – as indicated earlier, teachers are not very good at articulating their needs. (It may well be that these two things are related – i.e. if teachers had *time* to stand aside from the classroom situation with all its pressures, they might indeed be able clearly to indicate their needs very specifically. If you think this is a plea for greater support for teacher-release for in-service activity, then you are absolutely right.)

Classroom teachers and curriculum development

Greater involvement of teachers in their own in-service activity is necessary not only because teachers will learn a great deal from other teachers, not only because teachers working together will help solve many of our educational problems, but also because curriculum development (There! I do believe in it, after all!), if it is to be really effective, starts and is maintained *in the classroom, by the teacher*. So teachers need to be concerned not only as tutors for the in-service activities of other teachers, but also they need to be concerned with the analysis of their own situation – their own classroom, their own school, and the children within it. This is not to say that the national curriculum development projects are ineffective (although, in fact, many of them seem to be). Having brought a group of local teachers together to produce material for the Schools Council's 'Mathematics for the Majority – Continuation Project' (the design of which might well be very useful as a model for other national ventures), I found the teachers concerned, in carrying out their brief, also managed to engage in much fruitful discussion of their local problems, and continued to meet after their commitment had finished, in order to see if it was possible to produce relevant schemes of work for less-able pupils. This is now spilling out into a wider group of teachers who have become interested, for whom the teachers' centre has provided the necessary framework in terms of accommodation, materials, clerical assistance and other resources. Even if the Schools Council's Mathematics Project should make little impact in the schools (and let me say that even at this stage it looks like being one of the most successful of the national projects), the work of this group of teachers will have brought about effective development in their schools. Not least, because the teachers concerned are involved at all levels in the activity. They will probably only become thus involved at a later stage, when the centre has been established, when it has become 'a part of the furniture' of the area. Then (and possibly only then) teachers will 'drop in' with greater frequency and informally as well as for more structured activities. There is no doubt that the presence of a bar helps the more informal activity. Some ideas begin to crystallise over a drink. The centre staff follow up these ideas and they often lead to some quite significant work. This was illustrated about two years ago when, following a session devoted to primary science, one of the teachers was talking with the deputy warden and myself over a drink prior to going home, when she indicated that she thought there was a need for a nature trail, saying that while she had some interest in its production she was unsure about how to proceed – even how to start. We talked around it for a while and it was clear that she had a lot of ideas, but lacked some confidence. Eventually we equipped her with a cassette tape recorder, an instamatic camera and some film, and suggested that she go into a park near her school (we do have a park or so – even in Southwark!), and record what she saw, by speaking a commentary into the tape recorder and taking photographs of appropriate material. The results of this particular activity were not in themselves earth-shattering – but they were sufficient to give a stimulus to the teacher concerned and others, so that we now have available as a resource for teachers – nature trails suitable for infant children, junior children and secondary children. People tell me that this is curriculum development and I suppose they're right.

The teachers' centre is now building up a stock of such resources. These are particularly useful because they are locally initiated and locally produced by local teachers. This alone does not make them any better or any worse than the material from national projects for which the centre acts as an instrument of dissemination. The point is that material from local sources is often complementary to that from national sources, the latter obviously being at a more general level, whilst local material can be pitched specifically towards local requirements. Indeed, one of the most effective ways of disseminating project material is to relate it to the local situation.

Media resources

There are also many resources available to the teachers in the field of aural and visual aids. A necessary prerequisite here is for teachers to be aware of what is available, and how to keep it maintained in working order. We are fortunate in the ILEA in having sources of provision and maintenance which are first-rate. There is really no excuse in London for any equipment to be lying unused because 'There's no plug on it' or 'It isn't working properly', and so on. There is a department of the Authority which is ready to service and maintain the equipment in the Authority's schools. In all of the colleges and secondary schools (and some of the primary schools) there are media resource officers, whose function is to provide the resources (e.g. in aural and visual aids) the teacher requires, and in addition to provide stimulation regarding the production of resources the teacher may not have considered, but which might aid the learning process. They may be considered analogous to librarians, but they are concerned with non-print resources.

Many teachers' centres in London have a media resources officer attached to them, and the one who is based at the Rachel McMillan Teachers' Centre shares his appointment with the college, in the same way as the warden does. He organises a wide variety of activities in this field, which can be roughly grouped under three loose headings – familiarisation, 'workshop' and educational technology. Familiarisation refers to basic competence with the equipment in common use – e.g. with tape recorders: 'Which button do I press, and where does the music come out?' Increasingly, familiarisation sessions are being based in schools. The MRO (sometimes with other centre staff) will go to a school, perhaps over a lunch-break, or immediately after school – and will give six or eight, or however many staff are interested, an intensive session in the use of the (say) tape recorder that they have in the school. (This sort of thing is done mainly in primary schools. Secondary schools will have an MRO.) After such familiarisation some teachers are enabled to carry on unaided in the use of the equipment in the classroom. Others need and ask for an opportunity to explore possibilities with other teachers, with the skilled assistance of a media resource officer. This takes place in a workshop session at the teachers' centre. These workshop sessions often feed back material elsewhere, e.g. into the resources collection. If a group of teachers have been learning how to make 8 mm movie films, for example – the only way to learn how is to make one, and if what they make is something that might be useful to others, then it is doubly fruitful. A group of teachers who have responsibility for aural-visual aids in schools had been meeting over a period to increase their own knowledge and competence with the equipment. But what also arose from this was a decision to set up a communal resources centre, with each school in the group contributing some money from their allowance, and this group have now established a Media Resources Committee – examining and evaluating the resources available before deciding which items should go into the resources collection. (It would have been very easy to set up four years ago a formal committee for this purpose – but who would be on it? And how selected? Would it be effective? . . . I believe that this group, having evolved as it did, is likely to do a more realistic job.)

The other kind of activity in the media resources field is 'educational technology'. This started as a structured course of that title of some 30 units, transmitted on the Educational Television Service. Each unit dealt with a different aspect (initially the 'hardware'), and this was viewed at the teachers' centre by a group, who had immediate practical follow-up to the programme led by the media resources officer. (Those who followed the entire course successfully were awarded a Certificate in Audio-Visual Learning.) This aspect – educational technology – spills over into the wider activities of the teachers' centre and should not be regarded as confined to aural and visual aids. More and more, the groups that are meeting are being faced with such questions as – What are your objectives? Can you define them specifically? Can you specify how you hope to achieve those objectives? What will be the *content* involved? What will be the process? etc. How will you evaluate your achievement? Beginning to formulate such questions, and seeking appropriate responses are the essence of educational technology. In making decisions as to which material is appropriate, we might well find ourselves in the field of aural and visual aids. But that isn't necessarily the case – though *resources* certainly will be involved, and the functions of the teachers' centre in this area are more evident.

The professional challenge

That some teachers' centre activity may be based in schools has already been indicated, and this is likely to continue, especially as the centre becomes more 'a part of the furniture'. In Britain the theory is that the schools have autonomy in matters of the curriculum. In practice, there have been constraints on the freedom of schools – at the primary stage, there was pressure from an '11+ examination' which considerably affected (if not determined) the nature and content of the curriculum; at the secondary stage similarly there were (and are) examinations which have the same effect. With the spreading of the idea of 'comprehensive' schools, with the concomitant lack of need for a selection process at 11, and the development of different kinds of examination in the secondary schools, the syllabi of which can be school-determined, as can the examination itself, it could be argued that, for the first time, the British teacher is truly free. This is a freedom which we have to learn how to use. Along with it goes a great responsibility – e.g. if the examinations don't determine the curriculum, what will replace them? If teachers themselves don't determine the content of the curriculum, then the publishers of textbooks will. Teachers having the opportunity to meet in congenial surroundings to discuss mutual problems, and in the long term redesigning for themselves the curriculum in their schools, exploring various rationales and developments – this offers an opportunity for a great leap forward in which teachers' centres have a particular role.

The state of very rapid, and seemingly continual, change in our society needs to be matched by an equivalent change in the processes of education. If we wish to avoid 'Change without progress', then development in education must start in the classroom, at the stage where the children and teachers are, and it must proceed from this base in a manner which is realistic. There is a place for the dreamers, for the innovators – even for the rebels – in such a process, but they must be related at all times to the classroom situation. In order to achieve this, it would appear necessary – and not merely desirable – for teachers to be heavily involved and committed in their own in-service education. The part that teachers' centres have played this far is only a beginning. Hopefully, their continued presence will encourage the increase in the nature and scope of such developments.

8 In-Service Education and the Teachers' Centre in a Country Area

JANET ROSEVEARE

Cornish background

Cornwall is large in area, but the population is scattered thinly over it. The peninsula is nearly 100 miles long, from Land's End to the Devon border, and 50 miles across at its widest part, and less than 400,000 people live in the whole of Cornwall, with about 60,000 five- to eighteen-year-olds receiving full-time education. There is no university, although Exeter has an extra-mural tutor resident in Truro, and an Institute of Cornish Studies was recently established in Camborne. The nearest polytechnic is outside the county, at Plymouth. There are three Colleges of Further Education at Camborne, Falmouth and St Austell together with art schools at Falmouth and Penzance (the latter for part-time students only) and a College of Mines at Camborne. There is no College of Education in the county, though St Luke's College at Exeter has an Outpost for Mature Students, also at Camborne.

Schools are many but small; over 250 primary schools have

about 1,300 teachers in them, and there are about 1,500 in the 44 secondary schools, which range in size from a secondary modern for 200 boys to a co-educational comprehensive for over 1,500 pupils. Distances between neighbouring schools are sometimes as great as twenty miles. Only three areas have yet to 'go comprehensive', and the delays are economic rather than political. Comprehensive schools are a more obvious choice for a rural authority, and Cornwall made this choice some time ago.

The county is beautiful and the narrow roads are part of its charm, but travelling is always a lengthy business. There are few buses, trains are reduced to a main line down the centre of Cornwall with only two or three branches, and the whole of north-east Cornwall is now only accessible by car. Not surprisingly, Cornwall spends £500,000 annually on school transport.

Facts such as these have influenced the decisions made over in-service training for teachers. Teachers are comparatively isolated, both from colleagues in other schools and from access to libraries, concerts, plays . . . even from bookshops. Visits to any of these often cost both time and money, and all plans have to take these two factors into account. A teacher in a two or three teacher primary school and a specialist in a secondary school have an equally formidable task in trying to keep abreast professionally, quite apart from the loneliness they may face at a personal level. Teachers moving to Cornwall speak of an adjustment of pace, a 'changing down' of gear; some find the children less immediately responsive than those 'up country', though nearly all appreciate the warmer and gentler atmosphere of both weather and people. The difference of pace and geographical isolation present teachers with yet another problem, of providing sufficient stimulating work, and of preventing the general lack of pressure from invading the classroom too disastrously. In fact qualifications are particularly valuable for the school leaver in Cornwall, where there has often been high unemployment, and where it is also necessary to qualify for training courses outside the county.

Another thing to bear in mind is that Cornwall thinks of itself as not merely a separate county but in some senses a country; the county boundaries will be unchanged in 1974 when the local government reorganisation takes place, and the Celtic place names reinforce the peninsula's sense of identity which the non-Cornish at once mock and, I suspect, envy.

Since coming to Cornwall six years ago I have tried to avoid chauvinism, but I find myself grateful for the chance to identify with my Cornish ancestry; Roseveare is an old Cornish surname, and most of us have been farmers, Methodists and Liberals too. The Cornish are recognised in their stories and legends as a proudly independent people, and this has its effect on our educational policies: the glories of Cornwall are its beauty, variety and sense of identity, and its main challenge is the difficulty of communication, both within the county and with influences and institutions outside it.

The in-service strategy

This preamble is relevant to the problem facing Cornwall in establishing a programme for in-service teacher training. We are not rich, and butter has to be spread over a considerable area. The keystone of the plan that went into action in 1968 was the establishment of a residential teachers' centre, together with local teachers' centres. There were initially six of these and now, four years later, there are fourteen in all. Before 1968 there was a teachers' centre at Camelford in north-east Cornwall, one of the Nuffield Mathematics Centres. The headmaster of the host school and the warden of the centre brought his experience and tact to the post of Chairman of the Central Academic Board for In-Service Teacher Training from 1968 to 1972. We have been very fortunate in him, a primary school headmaster and a Cornishman who has commanded respect amongst teachers and administrators alike. His position as chairman will have suggested the main feature of the way Cornwall has set up its In-Service Teacher Training Scheme. The policy and finance is predominantly the responsibility of teachers themselves.

A working party consisting of Education Committee members and teachers did the initial planning for the 1968 launching of teachers' centres: there now exists a Central Academic Board which meets once a term at County Hall, Truro, and makes policy recommendations. These are passed to a small working party of Education Committee members and teachers representing the board itself. This working party in its turn makes recommendations to the Further Education Committee, which refers to the main Education Committee. This may seem somewhat cumbersome, but in practice an annual rhythm is now established and the policy can make its way through. The composition of the first body, the Central Academic Board, is crucial. Each local teachers' centre send a delegate, one of the twelve elected teachers (six primary and six secondary) who form each Local Academic Board. These Local Academic Boards are the governing body of each local centre, and the warden acts as its executive member. The fourteen Local Academic Boards are invited to submit recommendations for the Central Academic Board agenda; these are circulated in time for discussion, so each delegate comes having gathered the opinion of his own group. Voting is confined to these fourteen teachers, although there are other members of the Central Academic Board. These other members are the local HMI, the Exeter University Institute of Education senior lecturer who has special responsibility for Cornwall, three of the local teachers' centre wardens (elected from amongst themselves), the LEA Senior Inspector of Schools, the Organiser for In-service Education, the Assistant Education Officer in charge of Further Education, the Tutor in charge of the St Luke's College Outpost, and a representative from Further Education (currently from Falmouth Technical College). The intention behind this structure was to make the teachers genuinely responsible for the policy. In practice, I believe this power is only gradually being realised; the working party has the power to veto or sanction suggestions, inevitably so in a system where the ratepayers' interest are the concern of their elected members, but they have in fact been eager to hear the teachers' views and to further all policies that seem likely to promote the success of the centres.

The wardens

The main recurrent point of disagreement has been over the status and conditions of service of local teachers' centre wardens. The appointments have been temporary, renewable after three years at the discretion of the Local Academic Board, and non-superannuable. Each teacher/warden is paid £360 annually, but carries on as a full-time teacher. In some cases a grouping of free periods on to one afternoon, or a decision by the Local Academic Board to pay for a replacement teacher on one day or half day, has enabled the warden to have this time available for contacting schools in working hours. One warden is a non-teaching primary school head, two are full-time primary class teachers, another is in charge of lower school mathematics in a large comprehensive school and yet another is deputy head and woodwork master at a boys' secondary modern school: the post of warden is only advertised in schools in the catchment area of the local teachers' centre, so this variety is predictable. Another variable is the number of teachers served by the centres; this ranges from 69 teachers in one area to over 400 in another. Geography determined the siting of the fourteen centres. In several areas there is only one secondary school (comprehensive) and so on occasions several centres will join forces for a meeting of interest to secondary specialist teachers.

For the administration of the extra funds available for these meetings, the county is divided into four areas, and four of the wardens receive extra payment for the responsibility of co-ordinating the arrangements. We are always concerned lest these meetings lessen the likelihood of primary/secondary liaison occurring at the local teachers' centres, but obviously a sixth form physicist needs to go further afield to meet a colleague than does even an English specialist, whose problem is rather different again from those of a primary school teacher.

The financial provision for in-service education runs at over £55,000 annually. It is divided up approximately as follows:

Residential Teachers' Centre	£28,500
Local Teachers' Centres	£17,500
Other Courses*	£9,500
Total	£55,500

Residential teachers' centre

The large amount spent on the residential teachers' centre deserves some explanation and, perhaps, justification. As warden of this centre, my vested interest needs to be admitted, but in fact the centre's right to the major slice of the cake has sometimes been argued even more forcefully by others than by its warden. The Education Committee is justifiably proud of its generous provision, and perhaps the residential teachers' centre is the most visible proof of its generosity to teachers. All attendance at courses is voluntary (I remain officially ignorant of any 'persuasion' on the part of head teachers), accommodation is provided free, travelling to and from the centre is paid for in full (at 4·4p a mile for cars) and a replacement teacher is available for all primary teachers and most secondary. We allow for about 60% replacement, and so far this has been adequate. In some parts of Cornwall there is difficulty in finding a supply teacher at all, while in others the supply exceeds the demand. The reason replacement is not necessary in all cases is that a non-teaching head would not normally ask for replacement, and secondary schools will sometimes prefer to cover the missing teacher's timetable amongst themselves rather than import a supply teacher for the week.

The actual centre has a peripatetic history, partly economic and partly educational in origin. After two winters at Falmouth, then two at Newquay, it has just set up again at Fowey. These three towns are all on the coast and all in central Cornwall; we have been able to rent hotel accommodation at out of season

*This includes courses organised by the Department of Education and Science and by the Area Training Organisation, together with various other courses mainly in the vacations.

rates, to the mutual convenience of ourselves and the hoteliers, without an initial crippling capital outlay. It will also be appreciated that it suits the schools better, on the whole, to release teachers during the central parts of the autumn and spring terms, and to have them back in the schools for the summer term, when activities, examinations and social events reach more prominence. Since residential courses have to borrow local schools' specialist accommodation, shifting the centre prevents one group of schools from being inconvenienced for years on end.

The problems have at times been formidable, including, at Falmouth, the packing up of all equipment during each weekend, and at Newquay the sharing of the premises with 24 Blackpool landladies celebrating a successful season! Our courses have sometimes surprised the other hotel guests, perhaps the drama ones as much as any, though I have vivid memories too of the music teacher who learnt to use a VCS machine in the hotel lounge, and of the Cornish dialect expert with his tape recordings and maps and eight different ways of pronouncing the word 'cow': we took pride in fact that the hoteliers' children were transferred from their private school into the state system, and we enjoyed the amusement of the casual winter tourist who found himself in the midst of a strong midnight argument about 'the Integrated Day', or a visiting HMI who waxed eloquent about a mathematical conundrum, seizing graph paper from the barman to illustrate his point. Stories of the residential teachers' centre would include making overnight arrangements for two boa constrictors to be brought to a rural studies course and enlisting the help of a Breton Chamber of Commerce to find thick bamboo for a musical-instrument-making course. Last year over half the courses were fully or over-subscribed and we are experimenting in this coming year with occasional sharing of the premises with Social Service trainees and others. It seems a fruitful possibility.

The cost of the residential centre runs at about £28,000 annually, including teacher replacements, lecturers' fees and travel, teachers' travel, hotel charges, secretarial help and the warden and deputy warden's salaries. More than 500 teachers attend the centre, over 400 of them coming for the full Monday to Friday courses. The County Councillors have always recognised as important the informal contacts made at the centre, and have even spoken of 'half' the value of the centre resting in the increase to friendship and communication between teachers and teachers, and between teachers and visiting speakers.

The establishment, staffing, organisation and financing of the local centres has already been touched upon. They vary considerably in their emphasis and in the amount of support they receive from their schools. Some centres are open on the same two evenings every week, and this pattern becomes conveniently familiar to the teachers and to the host school; six of the fourteen centres have accommodation that is not used by a school during the day-time, except when a specific arrangement is made; the other eight borrow secondary-school accommodation by arrangement with the school. This accommodation is often comfortable and suitable (like the sixth-form centre in a new comprehensive school) but storage facilities are obviously a problem, so it is almost impossible for teachers to have easy access to a supply of books and equipment, let alone facilities for the production of resources.

After the White Paper – a new era?

We have been waiting for the James Report and the expected White Paper on its implementation for nearly two years now, and it has seemed unwise to reorganise our present arrangements if they would soon be in upheaval again. The waiting has probably been hardest for the local teachers' centre wardens. They are aware of the amount of work they could achieve with more time for the job, and, at one level alone, recruitment for local courses would be easier if the warden could visit schools during school hours; he could also cope more efficiently with telephone calls and letters if there were time for these apart from snatched moments during the breaks and lunch hour. Some wardens have naturally become eager to take a more positive lead in curriculum development, but their terms of appointment preclude this, and Local Academic Boards and LEA officers have made it clear that it would not be acceptable for the wardens to assume any such inspectorial or advisory role. The fact remains that there is work that needs doing, and that it only occurs in unco-ordinated ways, since it is no one's particular responsibility. Specialist advisers for the LEA only cover about 25% of the school curriculum, and the rest is left to individual schools, calling on whatever help they wish to seek; this leaves a sixth-form classicist or a head teacher considering the introduction of Integrated Studies without an obvious person they may enlist, apart from our hard-pressed LEA inspectorate.

Schools have, of course, never been able nor expected to have their educational policy making removed from them, and I do not mean to suggest that this would or should happen. I suggest that there is an ever-increasing flow of information and resources going into schools, and that a central place where these can be considered, together with the person who has the time and ability to collate, communicate and evaluate, makes economic and educational sense. The schools are under pressure from many directions, and any help that can be given to simplify the multiplicity of schemes, projects, questionnaires and such reaching them should be seriously considered. I also have faith in the ability many teachers have shown to become non-teaching organisers without alienating their colleagues! There has to be trust and respect on both sides for the appointment of a full-time warden curriculum development leader to be successful, but I am sure Cornwall is ready to take the step.

On the positive side, we have established a principle of the teachers controlling spending of their own centre's allowance. There has also been acceptance of sharing of equipment between schools, and I know of many instances of other loans between schools having arisen from contacts made at the centre. Our schools and teachers are certainly less isolated than they were. Some of the centres have members who scan the Education Committee minutes and present a digest to their Local

Academic Board. Questions are asked, and the decision makers are becoming more directly accountable; this is an indirect result of the centres which I find very significant.

The Department of Education and Science may well have given encouragement to the third cycle of the James Recommendations, in the sense of continuing and increasing ordinary in-service provision, but if there is no extra financial help to accompany the encouragement Cornwall might consider re-budgeting for a replacement of its fourteen teacher-wardens with a smaller number of full-time teachers' centre leaders. There will always be a need for actual meetings to take place in many different parts of a large county, so that teachers do not have to travel too far too often, but it is doubtful whether we could in the foreseeable future afford fourteen such teachers' centre leaders, nor would our smaller areas justify the appointments.

If the Department of Education and Science finds money to help the LEA's to develop their work for probationary teachers, Cornwall will almost certainly be one of the regions to adopt the 'four weeks on, one week off' pattern. The one week in five would also almost certainly have to be residential, and with over 150 probationers in 1972/73 we would have to treble our residential facilities, and find another £60,000 for the extra teachers needed. The in-service budget would soar from £50,000 to over £150,000, just to cater for the probationers.

If the 'entitlement' is implemented, it is possible that a good many teachers in Cornwall would wish to take the opportunity to spend their time out of the county, perhaps at Exeter, Exmouth or Plymouth, at the university, polytechnic or at one of the colleges of education. Not everyone would be able to leave home, and I think in particular of those with young families for whom it will of course be necessary to make more local provisions. It seems likely that the St Luke's Outpost at Camborne might be the nucleus of a 'professional centre'. The Cornwall Technical College campus at Camborne already houses the majority of our Further Education facilities, including the Outpost and the Institute of Cornish Studies, so a well-equipped and well-staffed professional centre there is an obvious choice.

Possibly the appointment of full-time teachers' centre leaders might dovetail with the setting up of about two or three professional centres in other parts of the county with less ambitious provision, places at which local teachers could profitably spend their four-weeks spells, or even a full term, if they wish to pursue local research, for instance; it will be remembered that the James Report also allowed for teachers choosing to spend their entitlement in industry or commerce, or perhaps abroad or pursuing an artistic interest: it might be that three centres in all would be sufficient to cater for the teachers left in Cornwall since less than 150 would be taking up their entitlement at any one time. It is certainly difficult to see how the Department of Education and Science or the County Council could find the £350,000 this would cost in Cornwall annually, but even a modest improvement on the present position would be welcomed by teachers.

The release of staff would cause particular problems to the smaller schools. In larger schools of, say, 40 staff, an extra two members of staff would enable absences to be covered without too much disturbance, but extra 'County Unattached' staff would need to be appointed to help the small primary schools, perhaps with one teacher working in a group of seven schools, if they had a total of 21 teachers between them. Theoretically one teacher would always be away 'on sabbatical' and need replacement. This new era is a trying one. We need to reorganise; we could afford three or four full-time teachers' centre leaders without increasing our global budget, but the problems require sums of money that could only come from central Department of Education and Science funds. I hope very sincerely that it may be considered quite an achievement to have reached our present position after only four years, and that we can look back on this somewhat static phase as the lull before the storm, or perhaps, more optimistically, a time 'recueillir pour mieux sauter'.

9 The Iceberg of Centralism – New Directions and Possibilities (Teachers' Centres in the Future)

ROBERT THORNBURY

Booking clerks for curriculum encyclicals?

What will be the relationship of the successfully established network of teachers' centres in a decade of expansion in teacher education with the DES, the universities, the colleges of education and the LEA's themselves? Some observers fear a binary system will arise with the teachers' centres as poor cousins to lavish new professional centres. Will the centres grow remote from the classrooms? they ask. Will wardens become booking clerks in charge of pillar boxes through which curriculum encyclicals are posted?

The *Guardian* newspaper recently questioned how long the spirit of centres could last when faced by the big battalions from colleges, LEA's and institutes of education at the new area co-ordinating committees. The James Report and the White Paper had effectively ignored teachers' centres. 'As usual it appears that educational reform is being implemented from the top downwards.'[1]

The neutral democracy and the responsiveness of teachers' centres to the needs of teachers have radically transformed in-service education. They represent the complex, sometimes illogical, demands of real people. Centres have not had a captive audience – and teachers tend to vote with their feet. But how long will the teachers' centre tradition last in an era of compulsion by stealth, when teachers become 'entitled' to attend in-service courses and encouraged to use 'subsidised' curriculum materials? Will teachers in the schools and the teachers' centres be able to resist growing pressures from a variety of sources towards the centralised direction of curriculum? In my view, teacher-control and public interest will provide the best safeguards against centralism. A clear strategy of resistance is set out at the end of this chapter. But from where, first of all, do these pressures originate?

The threat of centralism

The expansion of in-service education for teachers gives the government and DES nationally, local education authorities individually and regionally, headmasters and those who run professional centres locally – all in their different way – a powerful weapon for increasing the centralised direction of curriclum. With mandatory release, a carefully restricted range of course choices, and with subsidised materials it will become possible to exert compulsion. The time is arriving when, for example, the teacher could be asked to attend a course on a new reading scheme in his employer's time. Not unreasonably, on his return, perhaps with the teaching materials under his arm, the course tutor and the head teacher could expect the teacher to base his classroom lessons on what he had learned. Official pressure to adopt the approved reading scheme could be made virtually irresistible if those schools taking it up also received a handsome subsidy.

Since the publication of the 1973 White Paper, circumstances have drastically altered. New mechanisms for turning the classroom teacher into an automaton are to hand. An insidious spread of centralised curriculum could now be pushed into schools under the masquerade of inspecting what teachers have learned on courses. No longer will each local authority be compelled to write off, as a votive offering, its annual tithe of several thousand pounds to the Schools Council. That body, the DES and the public could now begin to demand classroom results. Events indeed have already moved suspiciously some way in this direction. There seems to have been, for instance, an assumption that the North West Project would directly alter classroom practice – perhaps because its budget had been voted by interested local councillors.

Will educational publishing decline?

Educational publishers and their authors could prove to be early casualties. Centralising trends have begun to deny the teacher his economic individualism and the publisher of books and equipment his traditional entrepreneurial role. Curriculum development was until a decade ago a cottage industry, conducted by keen teachers writing textbooks in their spare time on the dining-room table. Sometimes a textbook hit the jackpot and ran for generations of school-children and scores of reprintings. The successful writer, an Unstead or Ridout, was reputedly able by the 1950's to earn tens of thousands of pounds per year for himself and his publisher.

Now all that has passed. The day of the prolific textbook writer, hoping to make half a million pounds with an enterprising publisher has gone. Books become quickly out-dated. No longer can they reprint for ever. But more than that, the individual educational publisher, risking large amounts of capital on a new series or writer, is in serious danger. Educational publishing threatens to be displaced by a system of patronage operated by educational oligarchies such as the state publishing house, the Schools Council, the regional publishing projects sponsored by the LEA's, or other baronetcies such as the BBC Publications Department, or the educational television service of a large education authority. Even the largest publishers have sought and accepted patronage from national curriculum projects – where the talent-spotting and commissioning of work has been done by someone else. They have complained subsequently that their publishing expertise has been disregarded, yet they are not guaranteed sales as would be the case in Scotland or New Zealand where a new syllabus is compulsorily adopted.

The teacher-author and his new patron also have a vastly different contractual relationship. Teachers writing curriculum projects are usually seconded on full salary for periods, as we have learned, of up to seven years. Their copyright position is that what they write belongs to the employer who pays them. But what happens if a colossal sale is found in the world educational market for new curriculum materials produced by a project team? Do they ruefully wish they had gone freelance for a few years with an independent publisher? Is there a financial share-out of the unexpected sales bonanza?

Educational publishers seem to have been silent about these threats to their tradition. So far as I can see, their role has been radically diminished without even the compensation of guaranteed sales. Anyone who has witnessed the impact of a successful, centrally-sponsored curriculum innovation, such as 'Breakthrough to Literacy', on the purchasing habits of head teachers can be in no doubt that the writing is on the wall. We are likely to see a decline in the influence and number of educational publishers. The individual textbook writer will become an oddity, too, when a new curriculum sells only if given its imprimatur by powerful institutional patrons. The dozens of reading schemes at present on the market may, quite rightly, shrink to a handful. Educational publishing and its relationship to curriculum do need to be rationalised – but not so severely as to demand scrutiny by the monopolies commission.

The academic threat

The threat from those ousted curriculum barons, the area training organisations and associated bodies, is easily stated. The ATO's are to be disbanded and their budgets cut for not having done their job since 1948. They've been snobbishly preoccupied with making educational studies suitable for senior-common-room talk – and have woken up too late to their mistakes. It will be remembered that McNair wanted them to set up teachers' centres, but nothing ever happened. Outlawed from their traditional territory, the university educationalists have begun to eye greedily and resentfully the proposed expansion of teacher education. A campaign of innuendo has been begun.[2] 'Officers of the centres are thought to have modest academic backgrounds and to have been selected more for their empiric teaching skills than for their insight into modern educational practice', one writer murmured into the ear of the *Times Higher Educational Supplement* readership recently. Teachers' centres, it is alleged, are too concerned with routine and superficial courses. They're not equipped for work in the professional field although they may be 'useful enough to be absorbed into new professional centres'.

The role of university departments of education in the post-White-Paper scene will soon be known, following pilot schemes for the induction of young teachers in 1973/74. Professional centres will certainly need help from universities like Nottingham, which have been taking a special interest in teachers' centres. For professional centres will need to provide a diversity of short courses, longer 'sabbatical' courses (the one term every seven years), day release for the first-year teacher, consultative meetings and training for professional tutors, and support with curriculum development and resources. But it will be necessary to see that teachers themselves don't get left out.

Will teachers staff their own in-service education?

The changing role of the colleges of education will need to be monitored carefully, especially since there is to be no statutory move towards more teacher/lecturer appointments. Clearly, the colleges of education must be brought back into the real world. As one principal has pointed out, a curious *bouleversement* has occurred.[3] The colleges used to be the progressive innovators of curriculum reform. But in recent years the new ideas have come out of the classroom and the teachers' centres.

The colleges have been repeatedly advised, by their own staffs, to rehabilitate their public image by supporting the steering committees of local centres. That advice has not generally been taken. Mutual suspicion, or at best an uneasy partnership, has existed between colleges, the centres and schools. Covetous eyes have been cast by the colleges at the successful teachers' centres. It will be remembered that 75% of all college of education lecturers were in favour as early as 1967 of a teachers' centre within a college – to mend the gap between themselves and working teachers.

The James Report recommended that opportunities for short-term activities, presumably the kind that go on at local centres be increased to the tune of £5m to £6m annually, but it offered no staffing release policy. The White Paper further assumed that colleges of education would undertake two-thirds of all in-service education work with teachers. The remaining one-third would be distributed among university departments, polytechnics, LEA advisers and inspectorate, teachers and professional centres. Such an implied reduction in the powerful, neutral role of the growing teachers' centres must be regarded with dismay.

Local education authorities have varied in their support for teachers' centres. As the NUT survey showed, there have been considerable discrepancies in provision, especially between urban and rural authorities. Many educational administrators made only shoe-string provision in the early days of centres, putting them in existing establishments so that no public money was wasted if the experiment failed. Emotions were ambivalent when the centres' success story became known. Education administrators wondered, like the sorcerers' apprentice, what they had unleashed. They were worried that teacher-run centres might get out of control, and run counter to official policy. Then, as advisory staffs expanded, a different sort of complaint became common. 'We have had a lot of trouble with teachers' centres where the LEA's have tried to look upon them as their own outpost,' declared Alan Evans of the NUT in a *Universities Quarterly* debate on the James Report.[4] '. . . are we going to repeat all these mistakes again, with an LEA with too many PE organisers putting on a whole series of courses on PE. This is not the way to establish a professional third cycle of education.'

The discreditable record of the LEA's in involving only 4% of all teachers in the staffing of in-service courses between 1964/67 has already been highlighted. The revolutionary trend charted in Kent and Hampshire by 1970, where half of all the courses were staffed by classroom teachers, reflected a major improvement. But will this continue, particularly with the new longer courses? After all, it's more convenient to employ one college lecturer permanently to direct a set-piece than to organise a flexible course which has a majority of class teachers as visiting lecturers and where the course pattern each time is shaped by the teachers themselves. And how easy will it prove in practice for a teacher to have an individualised sabbatical term instead of joining a packaged group? A further suspicion must be that forceful LEA's might use mandatory longer courses given by lecturers in their colleges of education for indoctrinating curriculum policy. Follow-up work to courses, the professional support of teachers on their return to school, a neglected aspect of in-service education until now, might then be introduced in distorted form as inspections designed to twist the teacher's arm and make him teach the official curriculum.

Speculation along these lines is disquieting. For is there is one criterion by which a teachers' centre's success can be measured, it is in how far that centre has promoted courses and curriculum experiment led by talented, classroom teachers. The leader of the major teachers' union, the NUT, who has declared himself in favour of mandatory in-service courses, may inadvertently have put the teaching profession's head in a noose. How far teachers staff their own in-service courses is of course highly relevant to any claim to be a profession governed in future by a Teaching Council.

Professional divisiveness?

Many local education authorities, especially in the major cities, have evolved a dual system of teachers' centres. A network of general purpose centres serving geographical districts is linked with a scatter of specialist centres each serving all the teachers in one subject. This often works well. Both specialist and general purpose centres often serve primary and secondary teachers. But this pattern can become professionally divisive in some circumstances. For instance, as we saw at York, the prestigious curriculum development, or specialist centre, and the poor cousin, the general in-service centre, can become institutionalised in different buildings with separate notice-boards.

The binary danger that exists here is easy to see. All teachers could in the future be divided up into curriculum development sheep working at specialist centres and in-service goats sent to courses at general-purpose centres. Another danger, already apparent in some authorities, is that specialist centres will pursue a policy of working exclusively with secondary teachers. Moreover, there is an increasing tendency for specialist centres in curriculum development to be directly controlled by the LEA advisers or inspectorate who may or may not consult teachers in determining the programme.

Administrative apartheid along these lines could be mistakenly represented as White Paper policy. 'Professional Centres' would then be concerned with statutory in-service and induction courses for teachers released from their schools, curriculum development for secondary teachers, and courses of an academic, professional kind for which creditation could be awarded by the responsible people, inspectors and college or university lecturers, who staffed and directed them. Teachers' centres, relying on voluntary attendance and concentrating on the day-to-day support of the teachers in the schools, would offer guitar classes, tips on teaching and group therapy for primary teachers and no professional qualifications. With low prestige and a shoe-string budget they could in consequence be safely left to be run by the teachers themselves. General purpose centres might be used, the warden acting as a booking clerk, as occasional venues for 'professional centre' activity. It would not be separate buildings, but such labels as 'the mode of activity', which would mask this bland sabotage of traditions so recently established by teachers' centres.

Teachers' centres and specialisms

Should there be specialist centres or centres with specialisms? I think the danger of a split in the teaching community can be best avoided by an open approach to this question. Undoubtedly, high-powered regional or even national professional centres will emerge, like the one specialising in the teaching of reading at Reading, perhaps employing specialist staff. But in general, specialist centres should be set up to solve their curriculum development problems and their role altered when the job is completed.

Often, quite spontaneously, specialisms develop at general purpose centres. A problem is identified. Responding to requests by teachers or others, the local centre puts on a programme of courses and meetings on that topic. Sometimes enough new original ideas and initiatives are generated for a curriculum development working party to form, which the centre then supports with resources and staffing. A specialist bias in a centre's work is often related to the warden's own background and expertise. He may even have been appointed with an emphasis on development work in that specialism in mind.

At my own centre, four years of curriculum development activity have concentrated largely on the teaching of reading. My own teaching experience, local expertise from the United Kingdom Reading Association branch, enthusiasm from the inspectors, general professional concern about the reading standards of London children, and keen interest on the part of the headmaster and staff whose building we share – these were the key factors in our building up a collaborative reading workshop within the school. Our reading workshop now offers a full programme of specialist courses on reading to West London teachers, contributes to a six-week full-time course on literacy held in the teachers' centre, and is a study centre for the Open University post-experience course on the Teaching of Reading, tutored by the warden. Material produced in the workshop by teachers has been presented to the Bullock Committee on the teaching of reading, we receive many visitors, especially student teachers, and the reading workshop has made video- and slide-tape programmes for the Open University and for in-service courses for London teachers, as well as maintaining good contact with specialist centres engaged in similar work.

Conversely, as Geoffrey Matthews shows in his chapter, it often happens that a specialist centre, like so many of the Nuffield Mathematics Project workshops, will diversify its role to become a multi-purpose centre.

A growing interest at present is in the idea of teachers' centres specialising as local resource centres, as sub-stations in the national resources grid, possessing a collection of loan materials and providing an information service. Schools all over the country have begun to experiment with the local sharing of resources, assisted by teachers' centres. Some centres, as at Leeds, have developed loan services. Resources for the classroom are increasingly being made in teachers' centres by working groups or individual teachers. 'Oxfordshire is now pioneering a network experiment in which three teachers linked by a central communications centre, making available a range of locally produced non-book resources to schools as part of their work in stimulating curriculum revision and resources production'.[5] Sometimes the result is worth copying on a large scale for other teachers. The setting up of a Media Resources Centre and publishing enterprise in inner London has already been mentioned. Audio-visual-aids programmes on the teaching of reading, written by local teachers at my own centre, have been given full-scale manufacture there and made available to all London teachers. The school librarian and media resources officer become 'curriculum influentials' in this expanding situation, for they alone are trained to handle the encyclopaedic range of curriculum resources.

Centres and courses in schools – the Titanic syndrome

Teachers' centres sited in schools have received a mixed press.

I am in no doubt that there is a need for the comfortable centre where teachers can relax away from the classroom. As we saw, the installation of teachers' centres in existing primary schools in Surrey was not entirely satisfactory. On the other hand, I have found, there are advantages of professional credibility and 'being able to keep your finger on the pulse of what teachers are doing' for the warden whose centre is in a school. Our reading workshop, run in collaboration with the school, would be a book museum without the lively children who work there with staff and visitors. A good principle to follow in in-service support is to site resources and staff at the most local point – in the school or teachers' centre.

There are as well a number of cogent arguments for encouraging school-based courses and curriculum development activity. It is sensible to send repeat courses out on tour away from the teachers' centre so that an entirely different group of people can attend. Large schools can often offer superior facilities such as a pottery kiln or theatre. A large staff room can often recruit enough teachers to fill a course and there is then an increased chance that a core of enthusiasts may introduce the new approach in that school. Rush-hour travel or a long journey across country may also be avoided by holding a course in a school.

Teachers enjoy visiting other shools and displaying their achievements to colleagues. Observing children at work can be of great value, we have found, and a single school visit can often contribute as much as a short course. In my own district we organise regular open mornings at different schools. Links between all the primary and secondary teachers in a locality can often be improved by holding a school-based meeting on problems of that neighbourhood. Sometimes a group of schools may form a curriculum development working party. Finally, when a centre expands its work the premises may simply become too small and then courses have to be held in schools.

Some secondary education experts have asserted that 'the individual school is the best unit on in-service training and curriculum change'. They argue that individuals and groups can be enriched by taking part in courses, workshops and discussions in teachers' centres only if attendance is an 'outcome of agreed programmes within the school'.[6] The headmaster of the well-known Thomas Calton comprehensive school in London has written about problems arising over travel and release when teachers attend courses at colleges or teachers' centres. 'School-based in-service training sessions, learning within one's own teaching environment, would do much more to help to encourage young teachers – and young heads – to adopt a more positive attitude to re-gearing and revitalising teaching techniques.'[7]

Secondary school head teachers have been rightly concerned to protect social cohesion and maintain control of curriculum inside the large school, especially where curriculum policy is already internally-shared with a collegial staff room.

Generally speaking, it does seem appropriate that secondary teachers should undertake most of their in-service education inside the school, and attend specialist centres or subject associations meetings which take them out of the neighbourhood. Nevertheless, the lack of involvement of secondary teachers in teachers' centre activities, which is universally reported, could prove professionally divisive. It will be remembered that Walton thought secondary teachers stayed away from centres to avoid identification with their low-status primary colleagues. In large schools the *Titanic* syndrome is also at work. Secondary teachers disappear each afternoon into a vortex of after-school bureaucracy. It is difficult to persuade them, like the crew of the *Titanic,* that they may not be inviolably self-sufficient, that there is a world outside which includes colleagues who work just down the road – or that the iceberg of centralism may be drifting towards them.

With the advent of professional tutors this issue will be sharpened. For will the professional tutor acting as a school-based warden in a large school only advise colleagues, and support and assess young teachers, in his own school? Or will he act as a tutor in other schools, and other types of schools in the neighbourhood, assessing new teachers for registration and giving them professional support? Whatever the pattern, many of us would like to see links intensified between the secondary schools, primary schools and teachers' centres. For the real threat to the large schools and their curriculum is the set of pressures towards centralism against which the vigorous local centre acts as an important bulwark.

Flexible creditation needed

There is another weapon, creditation, the award of paper qualifications for in-service activity, which might also be manipulated by those intent on centralising curriculum. Anxiety to create a respectable, easily administered system of creditation could lead to an inflexible emphasis on measurable, academic courses.

The problems should not be evaded. How can those aspects of teachers' centre activity be measured which are not easy to quantify for marksheets? How can in-service activity in an art-workshop be credited, for instance, where personal satisfaction, informal liaison between teachers, professional skills and voluntary attendance are all factors in any assessment? How far can a sabbatical term spent by a careers teacher in industry be counted towards a further professional qualification? How will an individual teacher's contribution to a team project in curriculum development be measured? How far will account be taken of the tendency of city teachers working under stress to make in-service choices which give them a rest, rather than high-powered courses demanding intensive effort? Insensitive compulsion might return these teachers to the schools experts in psycho-linguistics and even equipped to teach phonics – but stretched to the point of personal collapse.

In-service education, the professional support of the teacher, is a continuum in the decaying urban areas where teacher stress is great and complete breakdown not unusual. In the cities in-service education often means helping a creaking system to hold together. Teachers' centres, avoiding parochialism or condescension, must support the social cohesion of the schools and the local professional community – and the in-service activities undertaken by urban teachers must be given flexible recognition.

Above all, we need to play fair by those teachers of young children, who are the heaviest users of teachers' centres. Traditionally tackling their in-service education in short, after-school courses, primary teachers have been at a disadvantage. Their secondary colleagues seconded to full-time courses, or studying part-time for degrees, have received paper qualifications, promotion and additional salary. Even more unfairly, the longer courses patronised most by secondary teachers have had little visible impact on the classroom, whereas the classroom of the English primary teacher, polishing her professional skills unrewarded, had by the 1960's become a place of educational pilgrimage. Her work must, in the future, be given the professional credit it deserves.

Rigidity in confining recognition to substantial, longer academic courses, could straitjacket the work both of the schools and the teachers' centres. The time has come, with the introduction of professional centres, for teachers to log their in-service hours like airline pilots. Cumulative credits must lead to further, major professional qualifications. The devising of a flexible system should not be difficult for an education profession which has perfected continuous assessment examinations and the enlightened Open University Degree.

The way ahead was correctly forecast by D. J. Johnston, as early as 1969. 'With the imminent emergence of the Open University, with arrangements for courses fitting into a modified credit structure, the possibility is clearly open for the practice of accumulating credits to spread.'[8] He was right. As we saw, in Wigan the Open University actually moved into the teachers' centre. In setting up its first post-experience courses for teachers, the Open University has used six London teachers' centres, including my own, as study centres. These post-experience courses will each count for half a credit towards the eight credits needed for an Open University arts degree.

Creditation, a powerful weapon for centralism, must however be flexibly extended and not abused. The Open University's degrees have been eagerly sought after, giving it some claim to being the school-teachers' university. (Half of the first wave of graduates in 1973 were teachers.) Nationally valid, professional qualifications, such as the Open University will offer in the teaching of reading, must not be used for the centralised manipulation of teachers and the curriculum. Classroom teachers must not become marionettes jerked by strings operated from behind the scenes at Great Portland Street, Walton Hall, Hamilton House, County Hall, or even Whitehall.

Schools Council closed shop

The attitudes of the professional associations towards teachers' centres have fluctuated wildly. They have been sometimes enthusiastic, occasionally downright hostile, even 'blacking' the Burnley centre; but they have usually settled for compliant apathy. Teacher-politicians are not noted for their progressive views on curriculum. Understandably, for they do not have the time. English schools, unlike industry, have no full-time shop stewards, union work is done at weekends and evenings. The teachers' journals showed little interest in the growing teachers' centres, as we saw. And at branch level, the view has persisted among union die-hards that professional associations are concerned with salary and conditions – not with curriculum. The belief, reported by *The Teacher*, that centres should be politically neutral has been widely held. Perhaps teacher-politicians could not see themselves dominant in that setting and felt that political energy could be more profitably directed elsewhere. Anyway, you don't want party politics in the parish council. Generally speaking, however, this has meant that the teacher unions have not asserted control of management committees of teachers' centres.

Whatever the reasons for this, it has been paradoxically the teacher-politicians who dominated the Schools Council from its inception, having a majority voice and representing all of the country's teachers in decisions about curriculum at the national teachers' centre, in Great Portland Street. No one now wants the teacher unions squabbling over the carcase of local curriculum, but it has to be faced, the old distinctions no longer hold. There has been a revolution. Every major curriculum innovation nationally for nearly a decade has been dominated by a closed shop of teachers, representing members of the professional associations.

Strangely enough, as *The Times* has observed, although teacher interests have been in a majority at the Schools Council there is nothing to show that they have used their power to push through politically-motivated reforms.[9] In fact, just the opposite happened. The Schools Council ramified aimlessly like a gothic cathedral. No one ever drew up an architect's blueprint for national curriculum and the tower of Babel at Great Portland Street grew to a multiplicity of nearly 100 unco-ordinated projects. Gothic romanticism even pervaded its attitude to its products. Like the painter it did not care whether its works sold or lay remaindered in the attics of bookshops; their intrinsic merit mattered more than salesmanship. The Schools Council wanted spiritual leadership of the teachers' centres but no practical responsibility in their running. It leaned over backwards, and even at times reversed in situations where any accusation might be levelled at it of state intervention in curriculum. Only after some years of blundering did it emerge at self-confrontation. Having failed, as the state publishing house, to undertake even modestly robust promotion of its products, it began to face internal criticism. Project officers complained that the coyness shown about persuading schools to adopt new materials was making it doubtful whether anyone was getting his money's worth out of the Schools Council. Were they to be tenor castrati chanting curriculum development jargon at Great Portland Street, or was their work to have an impact on the classroom? There was concern about what happened on the death of a project, when the seconded teachers returned to their schools. 'Looking back now I feel that from its very beginning our particular project in Leeds should have had its own demise much more clearly in mind', wrote June Derrick who had produced materials for immigrant children.[10] She urged LEA's and publishers to put more effort into disseminating project materials, if necessary by appointing full-time leaders to do it.

At Schools Council headquarters the debate ostensibly wheeled round the question therefore 'How shall we improve the diffusion of project materials?' But behind this euphemism was the real question, 'How far shall we impose centrally innovated curriculum on the teacher?' Should the Englishman's classroom, traditionally his castle, be invaded? Or could the assault be conducted, more democratically, by stealth? Whereever possible, projects began to have a guarantee of dissemination built in to their organisation. The Mathematics for the Majority and the Middle Years of Schooling projects both deliberately set out from the start to involve large groups of teachers, often in teachers' centres, in writing reports or producing teaching material. By this wooden-horse device, the writing groups often continued intact after the end of the project, large numbers of teachers through their involvement in the project being committed emotionally to introducing the materials in their schools.

Will Whitehall intervene?

Over the years the educational reformation presided over by a Schools Council run by a majority of teachers has diverged from the thinking of permanent officials at the DES and more recent Ministers. The happy collaboration which in 1965 permitted the DES to allow the appointment of teachers' centre wardens 'off-quota' has been replaced by occasional squalls. By 1972 it was not surprising to open a newspaper and read 'The Schools Council Now Facing Another Rebuff'.[11] In that particular case, Mrs Margaret Thatcher had rejected the Schools Council proposals for broadening sixth form curriculum. Also indicating a cooler mood was the DES decision in 1972 that Her Majesty's Inspectorate would conduct its own unpublished enquiry into teachers' centres rather than draw on the extensive Schools Council files. What now appears likely is that that Council's vague oversight of national curriculum policy will be replaced by a harder line issuing from Whitehall and the DES.

'It can be expected that from now on the Department of Education and Science will take an increasing interest in the highly delicate issue on what is taught in schools and how it is taught', announced *The Times* following publication of the 1973 White Paper.[12]

While in theory under the Education Act there is little that a minister and her civil servants can do – in practice there is a great deal. One recent sign that Whitehall will be taking a closer look at curriculum in schools has been the setting up of the Bullock Committee to investigate the teaching of reading and use of English, following evidence that national standards are static or declining. In a radio interview Mrs Thatcher has also declared herself sympathetic to the resumption of full-scale school inspections by H.M. Inspectorate, a practice dropped in recent years. Surprisingly, she may have the consent of both parents and teachers in any intervention. Professional and public demand for a hardening of the curriculum and sharper definition of the teacher's role have been named as one of the origins of teachers' centres.

Curriculum counter-reformation

Wardens are constantly lobbied by curriculum progressives ranging from the local esperantist to dance enthusiasts in leotards. It is true that substantial new curriculum has been introduced – for instance in craft technology or world history. But a lot of what has actually been going on has been the tacit revivial of traditional classroom approaches, dressed up with suitable neologisms as 'curriculum development'. 'Why, we were doing that twenty years ago, and now its coming back in,' exclaim older teachers.

Much curriculum development turns out to be what some teachers bitterly call 'reinventing the wheel'. Mathematics tests are out of fashion but there is warm support for courses on 'checking up' on mathematics learning in the primary school. Similarly, courses on syllabuses for the primary school are well attended as long as they are presented as 'curriculum guidelines' or 'continuity in the primary school'. One teacher's curriculum development is another teacher's in-service training.

Tautology is not the exclusive skill of the medical profession. When a doctor diagnoses lumbago, he is saying backache in Greek. The teacher fashionably re-christens in Greek as 'dyslexic' a child who cannot read – and proceeds to teach him by the time-honoured phonic approach. Students of curriculum development argot detect a remarkable resemblance between the modern 'integrated studies' course in the secondary school, with its 'lead lecture' given in the hall by a highly-paid head of department, and followed up by less skilled colleagues in their classrooms – and the nineteenth-century 'monitorial system', where a master lesson was followed up by assistants. By the same token, vertical mixed ability family grouping, with children of all ages working together, seems to be an Arcadian attempt to recreate the English village school in the central city neighbourhood.

The swing of the pendulum, assisted by trends towards centralism, has brought about a return to structured teaching and curriculum orthodoxy. Strangely enough, this curriculum counter-reformation has brought the self-confessed die-hard and the trendy progressive together in the teachers' centre. This catholicity of support reflects the responsiveness of teachers' centres to what most teachers as well as many parents want. Many educationalists welcome what is happening but, as is often the risk with counter-reformations, we must be careful not to get ourselves deluged in dirty bathwater in recovering the baby!

Community participation through teachers' centres

Teachers' centres in future must expand their role in relation to the public. 'What we feel most strongly is that centres could provide a valuable neutral ground on which parents and teachers could come together', argued two college lecturers in a recent article.[13] Writers have continually urged that any future strategy for teachers' centres must include a community role. The suggestion most frequently made is for an education surgery, rather like the constituency surgeries held by many MP's or councillors. This consulting-room would be open once a week for parents who wanted information and advice.

Since the Plowden Report it has been impossible to think of the school and the teachers as divorced from the family and the community. The popular move towards 'community schools' must be reflected on other aspects of local educational organisation; and teachers' centres, responding to what is happening in this town, this village or this locality of a major city, are well-placed to perform a community role. Already it is not unusual for a small borough to use its teachers' centre as a place for parent-groups to meet or for public exhibitions on educational topics. My own centre has promoted parent-teacher book fairs and courses as well as joint meetings with libraries, social workers, day nursery staff and community relations groups. There is a ring both of prophecy and nostalgia about current proposals that the neutral teachers' centre should become a local 'education advice shop'. For, are not its advocates simply reverting to the original McNair concept of an 'education centre', a focal setting for public discussion of educational matters?

It would be a natural step if following the Russell Report on adult education the contemporary zest for community participation was encouraged by drawing into the teachers' centres for some of their post-experience education, health visitors, social workers, child-minders, councillors – and, above all, working-class parents! In this way, teachers' centres could act, not only as a bulwark against centralising trends, but also as a buffer state – explaining local schools policy and feeding back the responses of the community, before that uninformed controversy so destructive of trust has an opportunity to get off the ground.

Fringe benefits for the city teacher

There is a second community role that the teachers' centre must perform, for the teachers themselves. Low salaries, difficult classrooms and an unprecedented spiral in house prices and rents have combined to put intolerable stress on the teachers in our large towns and cities. We saw how, in 1952, Birmingham established the Martineau Club, hoping that fringe benefits would bring young teachers into the schools and keep them there; and how some other authorities followed suit. That staffing crisis has now grown to the point of educational catastrophe. The GLC and other city managers have issued dire warnings about the flight of the young professionals of the middle classes, including teachers, out to the suburbs. Our city centres, we are told, will become black and working-class ghettos like the American cities, unless socially balanced community life can be regained. Teachers should not be apparitions with briefcases who appear through a hole in the pavement each morning.

This is a national social policy and housing problem. Certainly, it will not be solved by lavish schemes of compensatory education or urban aid. Meanwhile, young teachers work in the decaying urban schools and desert after a couple of years because of professional stress and the astronomical price of housing. What can be done?

'What I need,' one young teacher told me, 'is somewhere I can go for a cheap meal, and a drink, where I can have a bath and do my ironing! I want to have one good night out each week and spend three or four evenings in a comfortable teachers' centre or club, where there's swimming, dancing, a bar, squash and other sports facilities.' Students' union complexes, palaces of amenity, providing accommodation and leisure facilities for teachers, are needed. The banks, insurance companies and many commercial employers already make such provision for their staffs. Many colleges of education situated near the city centre will have, following the implementation of the 1973 White Paper, spare buildings or site capacity which would convert ideally for these purposes. Sleeping on the floor of a friend's flat is no way to start a professional career. Short-stay houses and bed-sitters, attached to teachers' centres, are needed for the new arrivals who have not found somewhere to live by the first week of term.

The inception of a network of professional centres, during the rest of the 1970's, offers an opportunity for educationalists to tackle with vision the appalling crisis facing the urban teacher in his private and professional life.

The warden's role

What in future will be the role of the warden of a teachers' centre? Wardens have been described as entrepreneurs occupying a nodal position and as dogsbodies whose duties range from making tea to summarising Schools Council working papers. We are told that wardens are master-craftsmen from the classroom, who have low academic calibre. Certainly they have retained a tradesman-like loyalty to their classroom colleagues. Wardens are skilled teachers working at a special task in full public gaze. They have been released from classroom duties and their colleagues resent seeing centre wardens turning the handle of a tea-urn or duplicator. For this reason it is essential that the warden be supported, as I have been, by an excellent secretary and other assistant staff. Above all, he should not be found weakly propping up the teachers' centre bar at midnight, waiting for his last colleague from the schools to depart.

The warden, or whatever he is called, experiences considerable role ambiguity – which he can exploit, complain about or ignore. He fits no slot in the educational hierarchy. The James Committee saw him as on neutral territory, independent of the school and the inspectorate. His flexible status allows him to assert himself as an equal in any professional situation. We are never quite sure whether he is a low-paid adviser with a building or whether advisers are wardens with no building and only five weeks' holiday a year. The only clear definition in a warden's role is his list of the schools his centre serves. He is aware that the attitude of the head teachers of those schools is decisive for his work. So the warden needs to be diplomat, polymath, caterer, accommodation agent, catalyst and consultant – and a shoulder to weep on.

A teaching council for all the teachers

What should be the future role of teachers' centres when set against their exciting but menacing overall context? There can be no doubt that, following the 1973 White Paper, the 'inspirational' phase of teachers' centres run charismatically by 'mendicant friars', has been terminated. The arrival of professional centres will see the system bureaucratised. Centres will be consolidated as institutions occupying buildings.

In this chapter I have tried to emphasise a shift which is taking place towards increased centralised intervention in school curriculum, by identifying those peaks of the iceberg which can be seen on the surface. Creditation, subsidy, mandatory release, dissemination by stealth, the streamlining of educational publishing, moves to make the Schools Council more cost-effective, the curriculum counter-reformation – these are all, on the whole, welcome trends. New mechanisms are available for educational advance and we must use them.

Nevertheless, there is a serious threat to the best traditions of the schools if the iceberg of centralism drifts too far. A neutral regulator is needed – and it could be the teachers' professional centre.

The most casual reading of the educational press reveals that teachers, like the community, want more participation. When every teacher becomes compelled to attend courses, many more will demand to have a say in what is provided; and it should not be necessary to join a professional association in order to have your views as a teacher on curriculum effectively represented.

The voting unit for regional committees controlling in-service education should be the staff room – all the teachers in a school. The whole staff of each school must elect a representative for 'in-service education and the curriculum'. That teacher should join others at the professional teachers' centre, where a local steering committee would elect regional representatives. On this foundation could be built a pyramid of representation, leading to the superstructure of a national Teaching Council.

Determined, oecumenical enthusiasm on the part of teachers to control their professional destiny through a vigorous network of professional teachers' centres is the only antidote to the coercive centralism which could threaten the system.

1. Hartley, Alec, *Forces for Courses,* Guardian, 23 January 1973.
2. Price, George, *How the James Professional Centres might work,* Times Higher Educational Supplement, 2 February 1973, p. 14.
3. Evans, Alex, *Teachers, Trainers and Development Centres.* Dialogue. Schools Council Newsletter, No. 6, August 1970, p. 3.
4. *James Report Discussion,* Universities Quarterly, Spring 1972, p. 155.
5. *School Resources Centres,* Schools Council Working Paper, No. 43, 1972, Evans/Methuen Educational, p. 84.
   See also Garnett, Emmeline, *Area Resource Centre: An Experiment,* Arnold, 1972.
6. Rogers, Guy, *Curriculum Reform and Teacher Reform in the Secondary Schools,* London Educational Review, Vol. 1, No. 2, Summer 1972, p. 43.
   See also Cave, R. G., *An Introduction to Curriculum Development,* Ward Lock Educational, 1971, p. 35.
7. Pepper, R., *In-service Training and the Thomas Calton School, Peckham,* Forum, Spring 1972, Vol. 14, No. 2, p. 50.
8. Johnston, D. J., *In-service Evolution,* Education for Teaching, 1969.
9. Jessel, Stephen, The Times Educational Notebook, Wednesday, 23 August 1972.
10. Derrick, June, *The End of a Project.* Dialogue. Schools Council Newsletter, No. 10, February 1972, pp. 8–9.
11. Jessel, Stephen, The Times Educational Notebook, 23 August 1972, op. cit.
12. Jessel, Stephen, *Whitehall expected to take a closer look at what is taught in schools,* The Times Educational Notebook, 2 January 1973.
13. Hubbard, D. N., and Salt, J., *Teachers' Centres – Some suggestions for a strategy,* Forum, Spring 1972, p. 64.

Supplementary Bibliography

Select Bibliography of books and articles: not including those already mentioned in the source notes at the end of each chapter.

BOOKS

Adult Education: A Plan for Development (Russel Report), H.M.S.O., 1973.

Britton, J. N., Martin, N. C., and Rosen, H., *Multiple marking of English compositions: an account of an experiment*, H.M.S.O., 1966, Schools Council.

Burgess Tyrrell, Ed., *Dear Lord James. A Critique of Teacher Education*, Penguin, 1971.

Burke, Vincent, *Teachers in Turmoil*, Penguin Books, 1971.

Cane, Brian, and Shroeder, Colin, *The Teacher and Research*, National Foundation for Educational Research in England and Wales, 1970.

The Certificate of Secondary Education: some suggestions for teachers and examiners, H.M.S.O., 1963, Schools Council.

CREDO (Centre for curriculum renewal and educational development overseas), *Modern curriculum development in Britain*, Credo, 1968.

Gibson, Rex, Ed., *The Professional Tutor*, Cambridge Institute of Education, 1972.

Hewett, S., Ed., *The Training of Teachers: A Factual Survey*, University of London Press, 1971.

Hooper, Richard, Ed., *The Curriculum Context Design and Development*, Oliver & Boyd, Open University Press, 1971.

In-service Education for Secondary Teachers, International Bulletin of Secondary Education, December 1969.

Johnston, D. J., *Teachers In-service Training*, Pergamon, 1971.

Kemble, Bruce, Ed., *Fit to Teach*, Hutchinson Educational Ltd., 1971.

Kerr, J. F., Ed., *Changing the Curriculum*, University of London Press, 1969.

Lawler, M. R., Ed., *Strategies for planned curriculum innovation*, Teachers college, Columbia, 1970.

Lawton, Dennis, *Social Class, Language and Education*, Routledge and Kegan Paul, 1968.

Lawton, Dennis, Campbell, James and Burkitt, Valerie, *Social Studies 8–13*, Evans/Methuen Educational, 1971, Schools Council Working Paper 39.

Lieberman, M., *Education as a Profession*, Englewood Cliffs, N. J., Prentice-Hall, 1965.

Parry, J. B., *The James Tricycle*, George Allen & Unwin, 1972.

Start, K. B., and Wells, B. K., *The Trend of Reading Standards*, NFER, 1972.

Support for School Science and Technology, Schools Council Working Paper 38, Evans/Methuen Educational, 1971.

Taba, Hilda, *Curriculum Development – Theory and Practice*, Harcourt Brace and World, 1962.

Taylor, P. H., *How teachers plan their courses*, NFER, 1970.

Taylor, L. C., *Resources for learning*, Penguin, 1971.

Tyler, R. W., *Basic Principles of Curriculum and Instruction*, University of Chicago Press, 1950.

Watkins, Roger Ed., *In-service Training: Structure and Content*, Ward Lock, 1973.

Wheeler, D. K., *Curriculum Processes*, University of London Press, 1967.

Willey, F. T., and Maddison, R. E., *An Enquiry into Teacher Training*, University of London Press, October 1971.

The Yearbook of Education (1953), *Teacher Education*, London, Evans.

The Yearbook of Education (1963), *The Education and Training of Teachers*, London, Evans.

ARTICLES

Bailey, D. (1967), *In-service training: a staff development programme*, Technical Education, 9 October, pp. 433, 435.

Bamford, T. W. (1964), *Students, teachers and teacher shortages*, Aspects of Education, 1 July, pp. 86–9.

Banks, L. J., *Curriculum Developments in Britain 1963/8*, Journal of Curriculum Studies, Vol. 1, No. 3, 1969.

Bar, M. R., Ed., *Curriculum innovation in practice in relation to colleges of education*, Edge Hill College of Education, 1969.

Barry, C. H., and Townsend, H. E. R. (1968), *Heads' in-tray exercises*, Education, 1 November, pp. 525–6.

Bell, H. K., *In-service training in Kent*, Trends in Education, No. 18, April 1970, pp. 45–80.

Breslin, William, *Curriculum Development in Fife Secondary Schools*, Forum, Spring 1972, p. 60.

Caston, Geoffrey, Schools Council, *The Schools Council in Context*, Journal of Curriculum Studies, Vol. 3, No. 1, May 1970, p. 50.

Contact, ILEA Teachers' Magazine, *Series of studies of individual Teachers' Centres*, 28 April and weekly until 14 July 1972.

Curry, A., *Teachers' centres*, Visual Education, August/September 1969, pp. 70–3.

Dalrymple, A. H. (1967), *A new trend in teacher training*, Forum, 10, Autumn, pp. 18–20.

Dalrymple, A. H. (1967), *The in-service training of probationary teachers*, Education for Teaching, 73, Summer, pp. 48–52.

Dalrymple, A. H. (1968), *Using local talent*, Trends in Education, 12 October, pp. 46–8.

The Educational Development Centre Review, available from the Director of the Educational Development Centre, Garrison Lane, Birmingham, B9 4BS (and many other teachers' centres publish duplicated magazines or bulletins).

Educational implications of social and economic change, The. Report of Nottingham Conference called in preparation for raising the school leaving age, H.M.S.O., 1967., Schools Council Working Paper 12.

Ellison, M., *Junior workshop*, Trends in Education, No. 22, April 1971, pp. 45–8. (Consultation between Shropshire primary teachers.)

Evans, H. I. (1967), *In-service training for teachers*, Teacher in Wales, Vol. 7, No. 21, pp. 1–2, 14.

Evans, Keith, *Multi Media Resource Centres: a cautionary note*, Secondary Education, Summer term 1971, Vol. 1, No. 3.

Exworthy, S. W., *The Freedom of the Teacher*, Dialogue. Schools Council Newsletter No. 7, p. 3.

Garwood, K. (1968), *In-service training: a new role for the colleges*, New Education, October, pp. 9–10.

George, R. E., *In-service training of teachers in Wales*, Swansea Coll.Fac.Ed., 1971, pp. 9–12.

Grayson, D., *With teachers in mind*, Education, June 1970, p. 716.

Heaps, J. (1967), *In-service training in the south-west*, Teacher, Vol. 10, No. 10, p. 11.

Hinchcliffe, G. (1961), *Repair and maintenance: a survey of teachers' courses*, Education Review, 13 February, pp. 83–99.

Hogan, J. M., and Willcock, J. B. (1967), *In-service training for teachers*, Trends in Education, 8 October, pp. 17–21.

Hubbard, D. N., and Salt, J., *Teachers' centres; some suggestions for a strategy*, Forum, Vol. 14, No. 2, Spring 1972, pp. 63–4.

Integrated studies in the first years of secondary school: some practical problems involved, 1970, Schools Council Pamphlet No. 7.

Johnston, D. J. (1964), *Teacher Preparation.* Paper submitted to UNESCO Expert Committee on Teachers' Status, 3 April, UNESCO, Paris.

Johnston, D. J., (1968), *Opportunities for further study.* In: Johnston, D. J., *School Teaching* (2nd ed.), London, R. Hale, ch. 8, p. 68.

Jordan, Jim, *Change through a teachers' centre*, Supplement to Dialogue, Schools Council Newsletter, February 1970, pp. 14–15.

Knowlson, Harold, *Forward to the Sixth. (Development in in-service training due to comprehensive education)*, Forum, Summer 1968, pp. 102–3.

Knowlson, Harold, *In-service courses for comprehensive school teachers*, Secondary Education, Autumn 1970, pp. 16–17.

List of teachers' centres in England and Wales, London, Schools Council, 1972.

Lovegrove, W. R., *Links between a college of education and the local teaching community*, Education for Teaching, No. 77, Autumn 1968, pp. 75–7.

Moorhouse, E. (1965), *In-service training in Oxfordshire*, Froebel Journal, 3 October, pp. 25–8.

Owen, J. G., *Curriculum Innovation in the U.S.S.R.*, Journal of Curriculum Studies, Vol. 1, No. 3, 1969.

Pilcher Paul, S., *Teachers' Centers. Can they work here?* Phi Delta Kappan, January 1973, pp. 340–3.

Probationary Year, The. Research and Development Project 1966–71, University of Bristol, School of Education, Research Unit.

Resources Centres at School and Local Authority Level. Speaker: Ryder, L. F., Visual Education, October 1971, p. 29.

Smith, M. P., Kingston Polytechnic, *Curriculum change at the Local Level,* Journal of Curriculum Studies, Vol. 3, No. 2, November 1971, pp. 158–9.

Teachers' Centres, Speakers: Childs, G., Smith, R., Davidson, M., and Braithwaite, P., Visual Education, October 1972, p. 41.

Teachers, Trainers and Development Centres: readers reply. Dialogue. Schools Council Newsletter, No. 7, p. 10.

Walton, J. (1968), *In-service education in the south west,* Forum, Vol. 10, No. 2, pp. 47–9.

Workshops for Ideas, pp. 8–10. Dialogue. Schools Council Newsletter, No. 12, 1969. (Well-illustrated short feature on teachers' centres.)